The Consequences Of Writing

Enhancing Learning in the Disciplines

The Consequences Of Writing

Enhancing Learning in the Disciplines

Robert P. Parker & Vera Goodkin

BOYNTON/COOK PUBLISHERS, INC.
UPPER MONTCLAIR, NEW JERSEY 07043

We dedicate this book to Nancy, Jimmy, Bryan, Peter and Mike—from whom we have learned so much of real value about learning and teaching.

Library of Congress Cataloging-in-Publication Data

Parker, Robert P. (Robert Prescott), 1937–
    The consequences of writing.

    1. Language arts — Correlation with content subjects.
2. Creative Writing. 3. Report writing. 4. Heuristic.
5. Interdisciplinary approach to knowledge. 6. Interdisciplinary approach in education. I. Goodkin, Vera H.
II. Title.
LB2365.L38P37   1986   428'.00712   86-14712
ISBN 0-86709-117-7

For information address Boynton/Cook Publishers, Inc.
52 Upper Montclair Plaza, P.O. Box 860, Upper Montclair, NJ 07043

Printed in the United States of America
87 88 89 90 91 6 5 4 3 2 1

Preface

This book is addressed to those teachers of Grades 7–16 who have a sense that writing can have intellectual consequences. Some writing, obviously, is done automatically, as a matter of routine. It is not heuristic in Michael Polanyi's (1962) sense; it does not produce new, irreversible knowledge for the knower. Other writing does. Other writing, somehow, leads to a fuller understanding of self or of some aspect of reality beyond the self, including the act of writing itself. Such writing is heuristic, and the knowledge produced is irreversible.

This heuristic writing, this writing which has lasting intellectual consequences for the writer, and perhaps for some readers as well, is not limited to any one school discipline or any one type of writing or any one area of our experience. It can occur in marine science, drug-abuse therapy, art history, or career education. Heuristic writing also has no limits of form. It may be personal or impersonal, formless or formed, conventional or unconventional, short or long.

Though our case studies are based on a particular community college situation, we think that the principles and practices they reflect have direct implications for a wide range of kinds and ages of students. Beyond the case studies, we offer some additional examples of heuristic writing from earlier grades and from other disciplines. We believe that these writings, together with the historical and theoretical discussions, provide a starting point for teachers who want to incorporate more writing into their teaching and who want that writing to serve as means for students not only to understand themselves in fuller ways but also to understand better the realities of the world that are reflected in the disciplines they are studying. In this sense, our book is not for those whose primary goal is better student writing. It is for those whose primary goal is better student *learning*, wherever it might occur and however writing might play an instrumental role in that process.

Contents

Introduction

Schools are "language-saturated" institutions. The people in them, students, teachers, and administrators, use language all the time. They listen, talk, write, and read. They also think and learn. Students, for their part, may think about the content of the curriculum much, or some, or little of the time they spend in school, and they may learn much of what the curriculum presents, or very little. In fact, what students may think about, and learn, is how to play the game of school, how to get by or get over, how to hate the game, or how to fail. Nonetheless, students are thinking about and learning *something* all the time.

So, also, are teachers and administrators thinking and learning something all the time. As with students, though, we cannot assume that we know what they are thinking about and learning. For all these groups, as well as for each individual within them, the *content* of their thinking and learning is problematic. We need appropriate evidence to draw informed conclusions about this content. Unfortunately, we have considerable folklore, but little appropriate and substantial evidence.

The same situation, we believe, is true for the relationship between all this *use* of language in schools and the thinking and learning that occurs. Apparently, administrators, teachers, and students alike assume that some kind of relationship exists between language, thinking, and learning. Otherwise, why would students answer teachers' questions (orally or in writing), listen to lectures, take notes, read textbooks and other materials, write papers and reports, discuss assignments with peers, and so on? At the same time, we have no real evidence of how anyone, from any of these groups, actually thinks these two operations of language and thinking (or language and learning) are related. They all seem to operate as if they understood this

1

relationship, but the understanding remains almost totally implicit as far as we can tell.

So, there are two broad questions to consider, and virtually no evidence on which to base an answer to either. One question is: What is it that students (and teachers) are actually thinking about and learning as a result of their experience of schools? The other is: What relationship do they believe exists between language use and thinking/learning in schools? Or, to put these questions slightly differently: What sorts of knowledge do students and teachers construct in schools, and what role, if any, do they see language playing in the construction of knowledge?

Both questions interest us, though it is the second that we address in this book. Throughout life, we construct knowledge from our experience of living, and we use that knowledge to live with and by. Piaget (and other constructivist psychologists and philosophers) would say, in fact, that we construct knowledge in the process of *using it to do or to make something with* (Piaget, 1975). We are also free, as George Kelly reminded us so tellingly, to reconstruct our knowledge at any time, and often we do.

Symbols generally, and language particularly, play an important role in this process. First, they serve as a *means* of constructing knowledge from experience. We use symbols, especially language, to transform experience into knowledge. Not all of our knowledge is constructed via symbolic transformation of experience, but most of it is. Second, most of our knowledge exists in linguistic or other symbolic forms. Quite literally, we hold our knowledge in mind symbolically. And third, we use symbols to operate on our knowledge. That is, while we can use our knowledge to do things within the outer world, we can also use it to work *on* our knowledge, to analyze, understand, or modify it. (James Britton, 1970, has made this latter point eloquently.)

As teachers, we are supposedly in the knowledge business. Knowledge is what our students are supposed to get from their experience of schooling, and as their teachers, we are supposed to be responsible for the getting. Can knowledge, though, be transmitted from one person to another, or does each person have to construct knowledge for herself through her active operations on experience?

These two positions frame one of the most fundamental educational debates of our time, and each of us, when we teach, affirms one position or the other. Each of us chooses a position and operates in our teaching *as if* that position were true. Some of us operate as if we have (or curricular materials have) knowledge which can be transmitted directly to students. We can then test them to see if they have received the transmission. Language, for those of us who espouse this transmission model of teaching and learning, is neutral, a medium only for the packaging and transmitting of knowledge which is pre-formulated and which exists outside of time and apart from knowers. Because language is neutral, a transmission medium only, those who take this view don't have to worry about the *relationship* of language and thinking except to fuss a little about jargon which might cloud the channel or otherwise interfere with the transmission. For the transmission people, just a little Edwin Newman-style carping and then they can continue on as if thinking and learning were language-free activities.

If, on the other hand, we believe that each learner must construct knowledge for herself through her operations on experience, then we must view language differently. Language must be seen as playing an active role in the construction of knowledge. In the simplest terms, we use language to transform experience into knowledge. So, *how* each of us uses language becomes a crucial issue. As teachers, we must decide, for individual students as well as for groups, what kinds of language uses, in what circumstances, best serve thinking and learning purposes. Putting things in our own words, even in our most everyday, colloquial words, does not debase knowledge and thus is not something to be barely tolerated for "weaker" students, but a necessary step for each of us in the construction of knowledge. Informal or personal or colloquial uses of language deserve support because they are useful, at least at early points in each person's process of learning something new.

Perhaps this brief argument makes clear our belief that each of us, in our teaching, commits to a point of view about how people know things and about the role that language plays in knowing. Which is to say, each of us commits to a particular "theory" of knowledge and that theory includes some notions about the role of language. Frank Smith (1982) says,

> In my view the brain must contain nothing less than a working model of the world, a theoretical model that every living brain has itself constructed for itself, with nothing more specific to work on than the cryptic neural bulletins it receives from whatever constitutes the world outside.
>
> This model or theory of what the world is like is all the brain possesses to make sense of the world. It has no other resource. (p. 30)

Earlier, Piaget and Inhelder (1969) described each of us as evidencing in all our operations, a "theory in action." We have and use such theories in all areas of our experience. None of us does, or can do, anything that is "theory free," so to speak. Every act emanates from and tests an a priori theory of some part of the world. And from this perspective, the theory-vs.-practice debate, which has been used for decades to rationalize educational anti-intellectualism, becomes a dead issue. There *is* no practice without theory, and no change in practice without a change in theory. When there is no change in theory, which is to say in people's actual, operational belief systems, there is no change in practice.

Theories can be thought of also as beliefs and as ideologies. Thus, books which eschew theory and try to score points by going straight for practice are, at least to some extent, dishonest. Their authors don't make their ideologies explicit. Thus, they negate criticism of their ideology, or at least make such criticism very difficult to undertake. This book is not dishonest. Nor does it pretend to objectivity by saying: "Here are the alternative views. You make up your mind." Rather, we state our theory and its historical roots in Chapters 1, 2 and 3. Then, in Chapter 4 we present case studies of students and their teachers which were undertaken and interpreted in the light of this theory. We think they provide evidence in support of the theory and, in turn, show it in operation. You are thus invited to criticize the theory or our evidence for its utility, just as you are encouraged to reflect on, to analyze, and to criticize your own theory of knowledge. Finally, in Chapter 5, we offer what we see as important implications of the theory and the case studies for teaching practice across the curriculum. Again, you may wish to criticize the implications we have drawn from our evidence, or you may see others which we have overlooked.

Either way, as you work on the book, through language and in the light of your prior knowledge, you will construct new knowledge or reconstruct old by means of your own operations on the experience of our text.

1

Writing
Across the Curriculum
Origins and Potential

The purely communicative aspect of language has been
exaggerated. It is best to see that language is primarily
a vocal actualization of the tendency to see realities
symbolically.

Edward Sapir, 1961, p. 8

Speech is through and through symbolic; and only sometimes signific. Any attempt to trace it back to the needs
of communication, neglecting the formulaic, abstractive
experience at the root of it, must land us in the sort of
enigma that the problem of linguistic origins has long
represented.

Susanne Langer, 1978, p. 113

To say that we have exaggerated language as communication is
to imply that we have misunderstood, in the most fundamental way,
what we use language for much of the time and why language arose
in the first place. When we speak, Sapir and Langer claim, we use
language much of the time to symbolize experience, to transform
experience symbolically and give meaning to it; only some of the
time do we concern ourselves, more or less exclusively, with communicating the results of our symbolizations.

The relationship of language to experience is, therefore, symbolic and transformational, not direct and literal, and the meanings
we give to experience are constructed meanings. Language is our
primary means of making those constructions. In this book, learning
and knowing are equated with the symbolic transformation of experience. To learn is to construct knowledge from experience by transforming that experience symbolically. To be concerned with the

5

learning or knowing process is to be concerned with the process by which experience is transformed symbolically, and to be concerned with the role of language in the learning process is to be concerned with the specific transformational possibilities of listening, talking, writing, and reading as we use them to operate on experience. A simple diagram of the relationship looks like this:

symbolization of experience ←→ learning ←→ construction of knowledge

For teachers, James Britton's (1970) chapter on language and experience provided an early and eloquent statement of this position.

> The ability to speak and reason are, of course, highly character-istic features of human life, distinguishing man from the other animals, but the point is that we have to dig beneath them to get to the root of the matter since both are dependent upon the ability to generate and use symbols, the ability to create representations of actuality. The world we respond to, in fact, the world toward which our behavior is directed, is the world as we symbolize it, or represent it to ourselves. Changes in the actual world must be followed by changes in our representation of it if they are to affect our expectations and, hence, our sub-sequent behavior. (p. 14)

This view, which emphasizes people's "tendency to see realities sym-bolically" and which, thus, assumes a transformational relationship of language to experience, underlays the early years of the "writing across the curriculum" (WAC) movement in England. It is this view, a basic belief of Britton's and of other originators of the "language across the curriculum" (LAC) and WAC movements, that Americans have tended to ignore as they jumped on the WAC bandwagon. For many American proponents of WAC, language is always and only *for* communication, especially language as a school subject, and so talking and writing are to be viewed and taught only as *forms* of communication. Students, so the received wisdom goes, need to master the forms of spoken and written communication so that they may be able to reproduce these forms correctly in school and in life. The work world, assumedly, expects form-*al* correctness, and the function of schools is to instruct students in these expected forms. Language, particularly written language, is *not* for making sense of experience; it *is* for communicating and for transacting business. As a result, schools are places to practice, master, and dem-onstrate correctness in the linguistic conventions most suitable for the marketplace.

When this "muffin tin" view of writing (Berthoff, 1984) pre-dominates, there is no room for "a type of writing which would give learners the opportunity to do something for themselves with the knowledge they [are] being presented with" in school. Such writing, Peter Medway (1980) adds, "would depend on a context in which students were taken seriously as learners with some stake in the business of learning," and "its forms would not be dictated by the need to test them." Claire Raimondo (see Chapter 4) calls it "a sense of ownership" of learning. And this is the heart of the matter: in many WAC programs in American schools and colleges, forms of writing rather than situations for writing are taught because of society's need to test students for mastery of these forms. This need to test stems from, and rationalizes, the view of language as being solely for communication. As a result, many WAC programs represent little more than fresh attempts to provide better instruction in the forms of writing conventionally to various disciplines. Writing in science thus becomes the science teacher engaging more directly in teaching her students how to perform better in the typical forms of science writing, or worse, the English teacher conferring with the science teacher in order to do a better job *for* the science teacher of teaching science writing. Precisely this language as communication perspective, as Knoblauch and Brannon (1983) point out, underlies Maimon et al. (1981).

They and others have missed a point fundamental to the original WAC proponents: "the linguistic imagination — the faculty of the imagination and its vehicle language — is basic to human identity, existence, growth, and being" (Miller, 1982). To understand the past or to anticipate the future, to have a retrospect or a prospect, requires imagination and language. Both retrospect and prospect are imaginative constructions, achieved through the symbolic possibilities of language, not the progressive mastery of language forms.

Will our students fail to grasp the full prospect and implications of nuclear proliferation? Of nuclear war? Of the increasing degradation and destruction of our environment? Of the long-term results of nationalistic, isolationist foreign policies? Of the reality of widespread hunger in the U.S. and the world? Of the growing gap between those who have the most and those who have the least? If they fail to grasp these prospects and their implications, it will be a failure of linguistic imagination, a failure of symbolic creativity, not a failure of correctness in spelling or punctuation or grammar or essay form. As Paul Connolly, Director of Bard College's Institute for Writing and Thinking, affirms, and secondary teacher participants in the Institute's weekend writing sessions concur, "students must understand that writing helps them think" (Schneider, April 1983). So, if teachers continue to ignore the function of language to make sense of experience, language as lived in history (Burgess, 1984), in favor of the use of language to master the forms of language, they will be major contributors to this failure of linguistic imagination. They will have failed to form creative alternative constructions of the purpose of education, the nature of learning, and the role of language in the educative process. In this imaginative failure, they will fail to serve their students' best interests.

Language Across the Curriculum: The Beginnings

The intellectual roots of the LAC movement lie in a prior set of ideas about language and about people: particularly in certain ideas about the relationships between language, experience, thinking, and learning. These ideas, which are based on human beings as symbol-makers and symbol users, will be developed more fully in Chapters 2 and 3 and illustrated in use by some teachers and their students in Chapter 4. Here, our concern is to sketch the origins of language and writing across the curriculum so as to catch the vision and the intentions of its proponents. For it is this vision, together with the ideas which provide both source and point of criticism for it, which we believe are crucial for American teachers to confront.

In London in 1966 a group of secondary English teachers, members of the London Association for the Teaching of English, began meeting to consider the role of talk in English lessons. Their concerns were specific and immediate. They wanted to know more about the role of talk in learning and about how discussion might be best approached and used in their classrooms. As teachers, they spent considerable class time holding discussions, yet they understood very little about *how* discussions might lead to or promote learning for their students.

Soon, two things occurred. One, they found the focus of their meetings expanding to include discussion of a much wider range of issues, theoretical as well as practical. In their words,

> we found ourselves discussing the relationship between language and thought, how language represented experience, the functions of language in society, different kinds of language and how they were acquired, the difference between talking and writing, the nature of discussion and group dynamics. (NATE, 1976)

Second, they found it "impossible to confine their study to English lessons alone." Teachers of science and then of other subjects joined their discussions, and soon

> we found ourselves talking about "language in education," or "language and learning," and finally about language across the

curriculum. We felt sure that language was a matter of concern for everyone, that if children were to make sense of their school experience, and in the process to become confident users of language, then we needed to engage in a much closer scrutiny of the way in which they encountered and used language throughout the school day. (Barnes, Britton, and Rosen, 1969)

What were these teachers doing, and learning, about the role of talk in the learning process? The answer, obviously, is different at different times for different people. Nonetheless, a statement by Mike Torbe suggests the experience that many teachers had at that time:

> I was able to turn my classrooms into laboratories in which, together, we could explore, experiment with, and theorize about learning and its relationship with talk; because it seemed clear that what happens in talk is crucial to the learning of the talker. For the first time everything was making me look seriously at what I'd previously taken for granted, and indeed generally seen as a necessary nuisance, and something I'd have to put up with: the talk that my pupils did *whether I wanted them to or not*. Once I saw its importance and its inevitability, I stopped trying to prevent it, and tried instead to create contexts in which talk became the way in which pupils did what had to be done. The powerful thrust to share ideas and to test out new thinking, and to do it in the most natural and comfortable way — through talk — was something to be used and built on, not fought against. The taping of lessons and the transcribing of the tapes — enormously laborious, but as rewarding as it was arduous — gave a clear picture of the learning events of the classroom. . . . The more I listened to the tapes, the less I talked in class, and the more my teaching energies went into devising contexts in which the learners' talk could take place naturally and fluidly, without my having to interfere with it. (Torbe and Medway, 1981)

Note the experimental stance that Mike Torbe adopted. Equally important, note that this work by Torbe (and others like him) was self-initiated and collaboratively undertaken. These teachers, concerned to know more about the role of discussion in learning, instituted a series of meetings to further their *mutual* inquiry. They were not just looking, as individuals, for better teaching methods. Rather, they were seeking a fuller understanding of a process as the basis for developing better methods of handling that process, and they were seeking that understanding in collaboration with ever-expanding groups of other teachers. In this respect, their intentions were less selfish and less narrow intellectually than is often the case for American teachers who wish to improve their teaching. American teachers often want to be given new methods, for themselves, and nothing else: no collaborative inquiry and no increased understanding of fundamental processes. These LAC teachers, in fact, came to see that theory was not only relevant to their inquiry but necessary to its success. As Britton has suggested,

> taking the broad view, what matters most is that teachers should intuitively behave in ways that facilitate learning. But their intuitive responses to what happens in the classroom are strengthened when by reflection they cumulatively build their own rationale for what they are doing. That is to say, they need to theorize from their own experience—not in a narrowly pragmatic sense, consolidating what has been found to succeed, but find reasons, ways to explain both their failures and their successes. And once they have begun theorizing in this way, they can selectively make use of other people's thinking, other people's theories, the evidence of research. (Britton, 1981, pp. 2–3)

By 1968, this inquiry had been given a name, "Language Across the Curriculum," which had been chosen by the London Association for the Teaching of English as the theme of its annual conference. From there, this local movement grew to national proportions, with the National Association for the Teaching of English adopting LAC as the theme for its 1969 annual conference. By 1970, the LAC movement also included a book of published research by Barnes, Britton, and Rosen (1969), and a book of theory by Britton (1970).

Within four years, a loose but effective coalition of teachers, researchers, theorists, and educational publishers had developed. In their commitment to LAC, they shared three broad concerns:

> how pupils learn to use language, how they use language to achieve understanding and appreciation of their experiences, including the curriculum content introduced in schools, and how language use influences cognitive development. (Fillion, 1983)

Though some individuals were more interested in one use of language than others (e.g., talking or writing or reading), LAC proponents from the beginning believed in the importance of all uses of language, both for their contribution to learning and for their contributions to linguistic and intellectual development. Further, they believed, all uses of language are *dynamically interrelated* in the contributions they make to learning and development. Uniformly, they opposed the separation or isolation of any one use of language from others for the purpose of instruction. For example, they opposed scheduled reading lessons focusing narrowly on skills divorced from purposeful kinds of talking, writing, or reading. They also opposed examinations of teaching which neglected to look at students' learning processes, especially the heuristic function of language in the learning of all school subjects.

In its early days, LAC was truly a movement about the role of all uses of language in the learning of all school subjects, just as it was also about teachers becoming learners alongside their students. It was not about how to teach students to talk or write or read *better*, not that LAC proponents ignored or rejected those goals. Rather, it was a movement which involved a shift of focus from teaching to learning, from improvement in the mastery of forms to improvement in the use of language for thinking and learning. Thus, it offered a new way of construing teaching, an alternative to traditional views and approaches. Here is one formulation of this position.

> Hitherto, our attempts to improve achievement have largely consisted . . . of efforts to improve teaching — the ways in which we present knowledge. This emphasis is natural enough since subject-knowledge comes to children almost exclusively as presented by us. We tell them the knowledge in person or through the books we provide. Even field trips and laboratory experiments, which appear to be direct experience, are stage-managed by teachers: the experience is selected by us, and has meaning only through the concepts and ideas we supply. So the quality of the presentation can appear to be the critical factor; yet we seem to have exhausted the possibilities at that end, to no avail. But what if we shift our attention from what we do as teachers to what the learners do? That is what we propose, and what many teachers are now learning to do for themselves. Creative energy which formerly went into devising new and more efficient ways of presenting materials is being turned with profit towards understanding what pupils actually do when they encounter, mull over and try to express new ideas and information. These are the observable processes, accessible to us largely through listening to what the pupils say and reading what they write; through attending, in other words, to children's language. (Torbe and Medway, 1981, pp. 22-23)

Writing Across the Curriculum: The Beginnings

In 1971, the Schools Council funded the "Writing Across the Curriculm" Project at the University of London Institute of Education. This Project, which began in 1971 and was directed by Nancy

Martin, marked the official beginning of the WAC movement. During its five years of operation, Project staff worked with teachers in schools, gave in-service seminars and workshops, produced packs of materials gathered from participating teachers, edited and published pamphlets written by teachers and Project staff, and wrote a Project report (Martin et al., 1976). In its philosophy, objectives and methods of working with teachers, the WAC Project arose directly from the LAC movement and represented a development from within. The first two pamphlets produced by the Project were as concerned with talking as with writing (*From Information to Understanding* and *From Talking to Writing*), particularly with talking as the basis for writing development and with the cofunction of talking and writing in the learning process.

By the mid-1970s, interest in LAC and in the WAC Project began to develop in other English-speaking countries. First in Canada and Australia, and then in the U.S., teachers from various places began to apply some of the ideas and practices in their classrooms and to consider the initiation of schoolwide staff development programs. In the U.S., for example, a summer institute on "Writing Across the Curriculum" was held at Rutgers University in 1976, the first of its kind in the country. This institute, which enrolled twenty-five secondary teachers of English, science, social studies, and foreign languages, was followed in 1977 by a second summer institute on "Writing in the Learning of Humanities." Funded by the National Endowment for the Humanities, this institute attracted to Rutgers 50 college teachers from a variety of humanities and social science disciplines. By 1978, the Conference on College Composition and Communication had chosen "Writing Across the Disciplines" as the theme of its annual convention, and nearly 200 of the institutions represented at that convention reported being underway with some sort of WAC program.

Interestingly, WAC developed most strongly at first in higher education institutions in the U.S. Not until the late 1970s did any substantial or extensive work on WAC begin to occur in American secondary schools, and even today little has been done in the elementary schools on any widespread basis. Interestingly, also, Americans have been concerned almost exclusively with writing, ignoring other uses of language, especially talking. To be fair, some reading teachers and reading scholars have promoted "reading in the content areas," but again with neglect of the important connections that reading has with talking and writing and of the ways that reading can be used for learning (Lunzer and Gardner, 1979, for examples of the latter). In taking up the WAC banner (or of reading in the content areas), missed two of the most important original ideas of the LAC movement in England. First, the notion of the dynamic, developmental interconnections among uses of language has been sidestepped in favor of the historic tendency to teach each use of language, directly and didactically, in isolation from other uses as well as from contexts of purposeful use. And second, the emphasis on the instrumentality of language, on language as a means of thinking and learning, which makes improved learning the goal of instruction has also been ignored, again in favor of the historic tendency to make improvement in correct use or in mastery of forms . . . the goal. (Parker, 1985)

Clearly, some teachers have developed new approaches to language which fully and accurately reflect the original vision and intent of LAC proponents. Just as clearly, some schoolwide programs have done the same, both in their staff development efforts and in the curriculum changes that have followed. Nonetheless, our sense is that such efforts represent only a small proportion of the total work being done in the U.S. which those involved call WAC.

What would a classroom (or school) look like which reflected in a full and accurate way the original LAC vision and ideas as they have been implemented and developed? Each classroom, obviously, would look different, depending on the age of the pupils, their backgrounds, the subject under study, the training and interests of the teacher, the kinds of resources available for learning, and so on. We cannot provide detailed descriptions of such classrooms. We can, though, answer a closely related question: What major "themes" would be reflected in the ongoing interactions and activities of the students and teachers in such classrooms? From the ideas about language and learning which have given substance and direction to the work of LAC/WAC proponents, we have identified nine concerns which suggest the thematic scope which the movement had developed by the time WAC first began to be discussed and developed in the U.S. Thus, any serious WAC initiative undertaken since the mid-1970s ought to reflect either a thoughtful incorporation of these themes or a thoughtful rejection of them in favor of an alternative set of underlying principles.

Two themes are absolutely fundamental to LAC (and to WAC in its original forms). They underly all the other concerns, we are convinced, and without serious commitment to them, the remaining themes can be implemented at best in partial ways. One theme concerns the role of everyday language in learning (both spoken and written), and the other concerns contexts for learning. Both interpenetrate each other, as in reality do all the themes. Obviously, how teachers view and respond to students' everyday language can be considered an element in classrooms as contexts for learning. At the same time, this view helps shape that context in fundamental ways, and if the view changes, the context also changes.

The Role of Everyday Language in Learning

By everyday language, we mean the kind of language we use when we talk to our friends, our spouses, our children, or our colleagues in relaxed and informal situations. It is the language we use to tell stories, explore feelings, convey personal information, apply values, and begin analyses of personal experiences. We use it when we have a comfortable, trusting relationship with our listener or reader. This language, expressive in function (Britton, 1971; Britton et al., 1975; Martin et al., 1976) generally follows the "contours of our consciousness," and in its use

> it is taken for granted that the writer [or speaker] himself is of interest to the reader; s/he feels free to jump from facts to speculations to personal anecdote to emotional outburst and none of it will be taken down and used against him — it is all part of being a person vis-à-vis another person. It is the means by which the new is tentatively explored, thoughts half uttered, attitudes half expressed. . . . (Martin et al., 1983)

Mostly, such everyday, expressive language is spoken. In fact, much of our speech is expressive. We do, though, write expressively on certain occasions and for certain purposes. We make notes to ourselves, write entries in diaries or journals, write notes to others and write letters to relatives or friends. This kind of writing often sounds speech-like, and it expresses our response to experience as much or more than it conveys information of one sort or another.

Moreover, because expressive language is our most comfortable, ready-to-hand language, we turn to it when we encounter situations (or information or ideas) which are new, puzzling, troubling, or intriguing. Being local and ready-to-hand, expressive language is also particularly "suitable (we would say necessary) for exploratory learning situations and for first drafts of new thinking" (Martin et al., 1976, p. 145). This suitability arises from two sources. First, in expressive writing the thinking done in the writing is the thinking by which a writer gets into a relationship "with a topic or question or concept." In such writing, the person generates her commitment to the topic as she writes. In the following piece by Christine (age 10), written as part of her science work, we can see her commitment to the topic and her sense of relationship to it as well.

Chickweed

The small leaves of the chickweed are shaped like tiny lemons, they hide the minute white flowers. Looking through the lens the leaves have the appearance of a lawn on a spring morning laddered with dew. Each tiny flower has ten petals and five sepals which are pointed making the flower look rather like a star. Each flower is surrounded by buds which are covered with hairs and when they all are in flower they look like little patches of snow. The purple stems of chickweed is sleek and is covered with tiny hairs which are like a baby's hair when it is first born. The chickweed is really a cruel flower because it creeps and crawls like a sly fox stealing hens and if it starts growing on lawns it will gradually smother the lawn. (Rosen and Rosen, 1973, p. 102)

In this next piece, Carol (age 13) is both generating a commitment to studying anthropology and beginning to explore the implications of what she is learning about the Waura tribe, especially in the light of some differences she sees between their society and hers.

Anthropologist in the Xingu

It is a very fascinating story, and I think he is lucky to be able to tell it. They could easily not have accepted him, and left him to die. It was very exciting for him I expect. I would like to be him, the waura tribe are very interesting. The Waura tribe know alot about medicens and stuff which we don't. We are ruled by machines, they do everything for us. But the waura are opposite to us, they have to get their own food. And make everything which they use. They don't use money, so they don't fight over it. They seem to enjoy life alot without using machines, they eat all different things as well. If you stayed their for a very long time you might not want to go back to civilastion. I think it would be good if people went to live for a year, they would appreciate life better. And might even find it fun. The waura tribe must be clever to keep alive. Because if most of us went and tryed to live like them, not many people would keep alive. (Torbe and Medway, 1981)

In both cases, the learning grows from the students' use of everyday, expressive language. If they were not permitted to use this kind of language for their initial responses to, speculations about, or reflections on classroom material, their learning process would have been short-circuited. Having to use, immediately, the language of anthropology or of botany would have set a formidable and unpleasant barrier between them and the subject, making it much more difficult to generate commitment to the material or to develop any real sort of thinking about it. For the most part, they could only have reproduced information in the language of the teacher or textbook without having engaged with the material or learned it in any permanent way.

This awareness is not limited only to teachers. Students can reflect on and come to understand the role that everyday written language can play in their learning, as this journal excerpt from a Western Australian high school student conveys.

> I found that with writing regularly, my ability to write improved enormously, not only in the quality of the result but in the ease of actually doing the writing. . . . I often used my writing as a thought formulating process. . . . The journal also helped me to understand myself and my place in life. . . . In a very direct way this better understanding of myself helped me to develop an identity and gain confidence in myself as an individual. . . . I wrote what I really thought and felt — what I wanted to write, and what was "me."

Contexts for Learning

No one knowledgeable about education would ignore or discount the influence of context on teaching and learning. This would be particularly true, we imagine, for anyone familiar with the conditions which prevail in many inner-city schools. At the same time, context is often taken to mean just the physical setting of the school: the location, buildings, facilities, equipment, and curricular materials. As LAC has evolved and been influenced by ethnographic research in education, context has taken on a wider meaning than just the physical setting. It is taken to mean, as well,

> all that surrounds classroom events including the beliefs and attitudes of the teacher, the way the participants in the lesson see the classroom events, together with those aspects of the school context which impinge on the teacher's intentions: in short, the whole environment for teaching and learning. (Martin, 1983)

The personal constructs of teachers, administrators and pupils, the systems of beliefs and attitudes "which underlie their behavior, and are the unseen prompters . . . of action," are considered to be as important an influence on the classroom climate for learning as are such surface features of the curriculum as programs or books or other resources (Martin, 1983, p. 144). These systems of constructs, together with the managerial systems of schools, are taken to be the two major sources of influence on teaching and learning in any particular school. As Nancy Martin (1983) asserts: "the differences [in teaching and learning] can be traced to two sources: a teacher's personal constructs, and the extent to which the managerial system in his school allows him to teach according to these."

Some of the best discussions of actual contexts in which students are actively, interestedly, imaginatively, committedly working and using language for learning can be found in *The Climate for Learning*, particularly the chapter entitled "Contexts for Language" (Torbe and Medway, 1981); in *Finding a Language* (Medway, 1980); in *The Martin Report*, especially the innovation schools (Martin, 1980); in *Closely Observed Children* (Armstrong, 1979); in *The Language of Primary School Children*, notably the chapter on "Writing" (Rosen and Rosen, 1973); and in *Communication and Learning in Small Groups* (Barnes and Todd, 1977).

The next two themes that we have identified concern students' psychological selves. They are students' intentions for learning and students' views of themselves as learners. In reality, all are aspects of context as well. When students' intentions for learning, for example, are more fully incorporated into curriculum planning and classroom activities, the classroom changes as a context for learning, and the same is true for students' views of themselves as learners. We have separated them simply for ease of discussion.

Students' Intentions for Learning

Those who teach writing with any regularity know of the difference that self-choice of topic can make on the quality of students' writing. When students choose or negotiate their own topics, they often write longer pieces, more vigorous and imaginative pieces, more coherent pieces, and more error-free pieces. The evidence is simply irrefutable at this point, and to ignore it is irresponsible.

Students also learn more, generally speaking, when they can not only play a role in choosing or defining the topics they pursue, but also in selecting the means to pursue these topics. When topic, means, and form are self-chosen or negotiated, the students make what they are writing about a more permanent part of their system of knowledge about self and world.

In this context, then, what is intention taken to mean? Nancy Martin (1983) defines intention by referring to a "spectrum."

At the one end are those concerns which cause students to write this rather than that in free choice situations — which concerns are often unrecognized until expressed; and on the part of teachers, the fostering of students' attempts to find their own directions in the belief that that is how the powers of language and thought are most easily gathered.

As those who regularly keep journals or do free-writing know, the act of spontaneous, undirected writing often "produces" topics. Simply beginning to write, even when you have no idea of what you want to write about, sometimes leads to or generates a focus for the writing. This may happen almost immediately, or not until several minutes of writing have been done. Somehow, in the process of recording what may seem to be the most trivial kinds of thoughts or impressions, more serious, more absorbing material can be brought to mind and developed. Thus, intentions to write about something in particular can be evoked or created by writing about whatever comes to mind at that moment.

At the other end of the spectrum lie "all the manifold deliberate intentions such as practicing comprehension tests for the exam, or writing a journal three times a week, or any decision to do this or that." These intentions can come from students as well as from teachers. At best, some will come from students, some will come from teachers, and some will be negotiated between teachers and students. When the actions and interactions of the classroom reflect a genuine mutuality of intentions, the teaching/learning process will occur in its most powerful forms, and the participants in those classrooms will experience the fullest satisfaction with their work.

This will be so because both students and teachers will share a commitment to relationships and to learning. The spontaneous writings of students and the support and sympathetic responses given to them by teachers will enable the commitment to a relationship to develop, and this relationship, in turn, will permit the negotiation of planned, long-term work activities to occur. Achieving full learning requires both sorts of commitments, and achieving both sorts of commitments requires both undirected, ungraded writing (and talking!) and directed, graded writing. When both sorts of talking and writing are valued, equally, and thus produce these sorts of commitments in students, you may create a school like the high school in Western Australia where, in Grades 11 and 12 at least, the writing produced by students, across ability, was found to be "varied, competent, honest, reflective, experimental, and highly individual" (Martin, 1983). That finding is so extraordinary that most teachers have difficulty imagining a school in which this situation could occur. Yet, it can. It is possible, and allowing scope for students' intentions and providing support for the use of everyday language for learning, as consciously valued and enacted aspects of context, can produce such a situation.

How Learners See Themselves

The premise here is simple: in order to be able to do something well, particularly when your performance is to be judged by external standards, you must see yourself as someone who *can* do that thing well, whether it be learning a concept in physics, repairing a car, or writing an essay for social studies. To a considerable extent, far more than most teachers tend to believe, the quality of students' performance in various areas of the curriculum is directly tied to their views of themselves as learner/performers in that activity or discipline. So learning, at least in the sense of improving performance, requires a shift or reconstruction of self-view in a more positive, optimistic direction. It requires a personal prediction of success, or the reasonable possibility of it, coupled with a sense of how to proceed, or what to do in order to achieve success.

This reconstruction of self-view does not happen in a vacuum or by magic. It requires action, activity, on the part of the learner and response from others, especially the teacher. How a learner sees herself depends considerably on how her teachers and her classmates see her. And this, in turn, depends on how her teachers see themselves as teachers: particularly what view they have of their role and of learning.

A powerful example of a student's self-reconstruction through writing was presented in Martin et al. (1976). We present the description here, in the teacher's own words.

> *The Magic Marble* is a breakthrough story by a twelve year old boy who had been very withdrawn and rather friendless. He wrote very little and with many mistakes. We were writing "novels" in his class and he wrote six lines.

The Magic Marble
Chapter 1
My name was Joe and I went to St. Georges School in Ealing. One Friday I was walking along slowly when I saw a marble. I picked it up and rubbed it. Then I put it in my pocket and started to walk along South Street where I saw my cousin Jenny. I called her. She looked around. I called again, she stopped to wait for me.

[The teacher continued] Somehow I responded correctly and he did chapter 2 — ten lines — and then proceeded to chapter 3 and chapter 4 till the book was finished at chapter 21. Each chapter was written on a new page. He was very shy about it and the whole thing took about five weeks. Since a story implies an audience I read it to the class who were most impressed. Then his father rang the school to say that Colin seemed very happy recently and thanked us. Since this he's been writing well and after discussion about getting speech down on paper his writing is now almost correct, and this applies to his spelling too. Now that his story has been "printed" as a pamphlet it's been used very successfully with pupils in remedial withdrawal classes. (pp. 124-125)

A second example, also dramatic, comes from Bryan Newton (Davis and Parker, 1978). Certain aspects of children's personality and behavior, especially those aspects concerned with school performance and learning, are strongly influenced by the social experience of schooling. Teachers, obviously, are at the center of this influence. Newton has this to say about their influence on children's views of themselves as learners.

> It is apparent from talking to children that their primary school experience . . . can leave a very strong impression on them. It is, apparently, very difficult for some children to respond to the school "me," to their teachers' views of them as learners, by rejecting or being critical of these views. They are what their teachers say they are.

Later in the same essay, after having discussed several students' comments about the effects of teachers' views and responses on their attitudes and performance, Newton draws the following conclusions.

> So, as we are concerned here with the pupil's view of himself as a learner . . . we can see a number of reasons why the model of successful learning presented by the school — and internalized by the pupil — is likely to encourage feelings of inadequacy in the learner:
> - it undervalues his experience and opinions
> - it undervalues his own language
> - it undervalues talk
> - it overvalues writing of a particular kind — factual and impersonal
> - it stresses a single audience for most of the writing, the teacher perceived as an "examiner"

Encounters with Models

From early ages most children are surrounded by print. They encounter it in their homes and in the world outside. From this constant and considerable experience, we now know, they build up knowledge of what print is, what it is for, and what people do with it. Before they enter school, most children "know" a good deal about print. They are, in a certain way, literate.

This does not mean that they can write or read fluently, or even at all, though more children than we think do teach themselves to write and/or read before they enter school. It means, rather, that they have constructed some knowledge of print and of what writing and reading are. This knowledge may well be partial and primitive, but they have it, and it forms the basis for their eventual learning to write and read. This preliterate experience and knowledge is also, as Vygotsky (1978) noted, part of a continuous process of development which stretches from gesture through speech to symbolic play and drawing, and then to writing and reading. So learning to write and read only begins abruptly and formally in schools, as a function of current patterns of curricular organization, and not in reality where they slowly and naturally emerge from early experiences and activities, becoming increasingly differentiated and skilled activities.

Thus, children become literate by encountering "thousands of ... different models of the printed language" (Martin, 1983). As used by LAC proponents, the word *model* does not mean something to be "consciously imitated." Rather, it refers to "an item whose use and form are recognized by repeated encounters so that we come to know, from experience, what it is we are reading" (Martin, 1983). We do not "learn" these models through direct teaching or direct application to reading or writing. Instead, indirectly, we encounter them and draw upon them, often implicitly, in use for our own purposes.

In order for children's writing abilities to develop, then, they need

> to encounter many, many models of the written language. From these varying models they derive their notions of what writing is like and how one kind is different from another, but we all advance from the known to the less known, and perhaps in many of the specific writing tasks we set children in school we don't allow them to take their familiar language equipment with them, and they therefore fail to draw on the experience of language that they already have. By demanding (across the curriculum) too much impersonal writing addressed to an anonymous public audience (and an adult audience at that) we are perhaps stopping them from drawing on their experience of many encounters with many kinds of language, and from trying out their own versions of these. Thus, the writing task is often more like a raid into alien territory, with all its attendant risks and uncertainties, than a companionable walk through

familiar country with excursions from time to time into un-known bits of the terrain. (Martin, 1983)

Two notions are crucial here. First, children need to be able to draw upon models of written language *for their own purposes.* When they are required to imitate a model directly, rather than draw upon it indirectly, and the purpose is the teacher's, not theirs, the result will be those empty, awkward imitations of essays (or whatever) that we all dread reading. Secondly, they need to be able to person-alize the model they are drawing upon, to make it reflect *their* think-ing or *their* response in some way. When the writing is required to be totally impersonal *before they have internalized the model or the purpose for using it,* the writing will also be lifeless, devoid of energy or vividness.

A Writer's Sense of Audience

Whenever someone writes something, that writing is under-taken for some purpose and intended for some person. The writer may not be able to tell you what the writing is for or whom it is for, but nonetheless it is purposeful and directed at someone. That per-son may be the writer herself, exclusively. If it is not just herself, however, if there is another intended audience, the writer herself will remain a partial audience. Even in the most routine, automatic pieces of writing, the writer herself is one intended audience, though her role and importance as a reader may be minimal.

By and large, LAC/WAC proponents came to believe that the best pieces of school writing, both as writing and as a means of learn-ing, conveyed a clear sense that the writer was writing partly, or even considerably, for herself as audience. Remove this intention to write at least partly for the self, and the quality of the writing suffers. Here is the way the WAC Project staff put it:

> We think it likely that one reason for the great amount of inert, inept writing produced by school students is that the natural process of internalizing the sense of an audience, learned through speech, has been perverted by the use of writing as a testing or reproductive procedure at the expense of all other kinds of writing. When a writer's focus is on returning as exactly as possible what he has been given, the sense of any other audi-ence, including the monitoring, reflective, independent self, dis-appears, leaving incomprehension, resentment or despair, or alternatively the satisfaction of producing something to satisfy someone else's demands. (Martin et al., 1976)

Central, then, to each writer's development is her evolving sense of her "monitoring, reflective, independent" writer self. For this kind of writer self to develop, she must be doing writing which reflects her intentions and which enables her to draw freely upon the models of written language which she has encountered.

This, though, is just one side of the coin. The other side is the writer's emerging sense of other kinds of audiences, of their needs and demands, and of the ways to shape writing to meet those demands. This evolution requires the opportunity to write for a slowly widening range of different audiences. Because both children and young adults do most of their writing in school, the teacher is the logical audience for the vast bulk of this writing. In order, then, for students to have the opportunity to write for an expanding range of audiences, teachers must, in our view, take three kinds of actions.

First, they must begin to take on different roles as readers of student writing, so that their students may experience and internalize these various roles. In addition to reading as examiners or graders of writing, teachers can read as partners in dialogue or as trusted adults (Britton et al., 1975; Martin et al., 1976). As partners in dialogue, they will be responding to their students' work as people who have a mutual interest in the topic and who share mutually in the possibilities for learning from that work. As trusted adults, they will respond as people who can be told things in confidence and who can be trusted to respond sympathetically and helpfully.

Second, they can create situations in their classrooms in which students write for other audiences, either real or imagined. These can range from peers, to partners, to other adults, to a wider, unknown public audience. And third, through the use of small, peer writing groups, they can cultivate and give status and legitimacy to peers as readers (and as co-writers). The efficacy of small, peer writing groups has been widely discussed in recent years, so we have chosen not to describe them here.

Conditions for Good Transactional Writing

Many students, perhaps the majority, have difficulty doing good transactional writing. The demands of logical analysis and logical organization, of appropriate use of evidence, of distinguishing between findings and conclusions (and other demands as well) seem to present especially troublesome hurdles, even for students who may demonstrate fluency in poetic and/or expressive writing.

In their work on the development of writing abilities, both the Writing Research Unit and the WAC Project staff viewed development "not so much in terms of the acquisition of various skills as of a hierarchy of kinds of writing shaped by the thinking problems which the writer encountered" (Martin, 1983). From this perspective, we must assume that different kinds of transactional writing pose *thinking problems* for students which are both different from, and more difficult to master than those posed by narrative kinds of writing. Thus, the move from chronologically organized writing to logically organized writing is a big one and difficult for many students to make without great struggle.

There are, though, some conditions which, when established as a part of classroom writing situations, seem to promote good transactional writing. The first of these conditions is crucial, and we present it in the words of the WAC Project staff: "Most of the good transactional writing we found in the work of older (as well as younger) students started from firsthand experience" (Martin et al., 1976, p. 152). This is not to say that the students had not made use of secondary sources, including books. They had, but typically they had consulted secondary sources *to extend* what they were learning (or had learned) through firsthand experiences like observing, collecting, surveying, or interviewing. So, the WAC staff concluded that "one of the conditions for good transactional writing is where circumstances reflect the interplay of firsthand and secondary experience."

The second important condition involves the creation of "opportunities for students to encounter . . . *varied models of good transactional language.*" The textbooks students read seldom provide good models of writing, whether the subject is science or history or mathematics or whatever. In fact, when compared to the best models of writing in a given field, the available textbooks often present drab, listless, uninviting models of writing in that field. As a result, students have no idea what vivid, energetic, interesting, provocative science writing, for example, looks like. If they have no experience of reading people like Loren Eiseley or Lewis Thomas or Niko Tinbergen, or even a skilled, amateur biologist like John Steinbeck (in *The Sea of Cortez*), they may unconsciously pattern their science writing after that of their textbooks.

We are not advocating that students be handed models of science writing to imitate directly. Rather, as we suggested above, these models would be read and discussed primarily for their interesting content. Only secondarily and indirectly would these models then be there for students to draw on when and where they saw fit. Regardless of the subject, though, it seems clear that students benefit from regular encounters with a variety of good transactional writing from various sources and disciplines.

Finally, students produce better transactional writing when they have a choice of material to be investigated and written about. Here, we are not talking about choosing topics for individual, isolated essays but choosing or negotiating projects which would require some kinds of transactional writing for their conduct as well as for their completion. This distinction is important. When the transactional writing to be done is embedded naturally and logically in a project which is either self-defined or at least negotiated, the writing seems to be less onerous and of better quality. It was exactly in this sense which the WAC Project staff advocated the teaching of *situations for writing* rather than *types of writing*. That is, they urged teachers not to teach and require isolated essays on set topics, but to require longer-term projects which necessitated a variety of kinds of writing, including transactional kinds, for their successful completion.

Assessment and Criticism

Evaluating students' work is clearly an important, if not major, activity for teachers. All teachers expect to do it, and parents and students expect it to be done. The assessment of individual students by individual teachers goes on all the time, and the incidence of assessment of groups of students through standardized procedures has risen sharply in the U.S. in recent years. Most states have mandated assessment in reading, math, and (sometimes) writing between kindergarten and Grade 12, and some have mandated across-the-board assessments in their public colleges as well.

Despite such increases in the amount of assessment of students' learning and achievement, debate continues about the role, the value, and the procedures of assessment—and of the criticism of students' work that often accompanies such assessment. Because this debate is so wide-ranging, so complex and often so heated, we can barely scratch the surface in this section. What we can do is highlight the issues of assessment and criticism which LAC/WAC proponents saw as most crucial to students' progress in writing and learning.

The WAC Project staff, in entering this debate, asked themselves and other teachers the following questions: When is a teacher's criticism or advice helpful? Need assessment be as inhibiting as many students find it? Does our analysis of the circumstances of school writing provide us with general answers to the problem? From the ensuing discussions, they concluded that "for criticism and assessment to be productive a balance needs to be maintained between a number of contrary pressures" (Martin et al., 1976).

First, the student writer's efforts to say what she wants to say in a personally satisfying way must be balanced against the demands of her teacher who, as a reader, is likely to be concerned about the mechanics of writing and the requirements of form. Both sets of desires must be accommodated through the achievement of some healthy balance.

Second, the writer's attempts to get her information right must be balanced with the demands of the genre. One of the biggest hurdles for students, as we noted earlier, is the move into the logical organization of material required by transactional forms of writing. Meeting the particular organizational demands of each transactional genre while, at the same time, getting all the facts, findings, interpretations, and conclusions correct is very difficult, and teachers must appreciate this difficulty and take it clearly into account when they assess students' writing.

Assessment and criticism that are too impersonal or too mechanical or too cursory, that reflect no sort of positive relationship at all between teacher and student, are more discouraging than encouraging to students and more inhibiting than helpful. This is true of young children who write long, complex stories at home and short, simple stories in school because, as one six-year-old said,

> I don't like writing stories at school. I'm afraid of getting mistakes. I don't know how to spell some words and I forget full stops. (Martin et al., 1976; see also Bissex, 1980)

It is equally true of high school and college students who glance briefly at their teacher's red marks and criticisms, only to crumple their papers quickly and throw them away. Criticism and assessment are most productive when they occur in the context of a relationship which has developed between the teacher and the student. No relationship usually guarantees no positive result from the teacher's marking efforts, no matter how carefully rendered.

Additionally, as many LAC/WAC proponents have learned, it is important that some writing be assessed and some writing go unassessed. The unassessed writing may be read and responded to but not marked, and the impersonal, formal writing will, at least eventually, be assessed. Even that writing, though, may not be assessed immediately. It may simply be commented on, by teachers and/or peers, and filed away until later in the term when it is reviewed and quite possibly revised for resubmission, at which time it is carefully assessed. This suggests that there be two major strands of writing going on in all classrooms: formal and informal. The informal strand may include, for example, journal-keeping, free-writing, note-taking, letter-writing, and interim report-writing. All these forms would be undertaken for purposes of thinking, remembering, learning, and communicating locally. The formal strands may include such forms as essays, stories, poems, reports, term papers, editorials, and the like. These forms would be undertaken either for the purpose of displaying knowledge or of actually informing or persuading someone of something. When informal and formal writing are *equally valued, supported,* and *responded* to by teachers, as Nancy Martin (1980) found, students know why they are writing and generally write well.

Becoming Our Own Experts

The spate of criticisms of public education in the U.S. which began in the early 1980s includes stinging commentary on teachers and the way they are trained. These criticisms, reminiscent of those voiced in the late 1950s and early 1960s, particularly take teachers to task for knowing more about teaching methods than subject content, and they recommend more, and more rigorous, subject matter training and fewer courses in "methodology." These rather facile, essentially political criticisms are, unfortunately, easy to express and easy to find public support for. And, like all such simplistic knee-jerk criticisms, they miss the real points of weakness in the relationship between what teachers know and what they do. As a result, they generate mindless "solutions" which solve nothing, serving only to advance a few individual careers at the expense of teachers, students, parents, and society.

The most serious weakness in teaching (and thus teacher training) is not the imbalance between subject knowledge and method knowledge, though some teachers know a great deal about one or the other, or both, and others know little about one or the other, or both. It is the view teachers have of themselves as curriculum technicians rather than curriculum constructors. "Show me the curriculum guide, and I'll teach it" is the attitude many teachers have these days, and the expectation most administrators, boards of education, and communities have for them. Teachers do not see themselves as responsible for deciding what to teach as well as how to teach it. They eschew the important, intellectual decisions about content and values for the less important, technical decisions and methods. They do not approach the job of teaching as if it were their professional right and obligation to make *both* sorts of decisions and, thus, to be responsible for knowing about their subjects, about students' learning processes, and about ways of teaching as well. As a further result of this self-perspective, they do not feel responsible, either, for constantly *learning more* about each of these areas, for being regular inquirers into these matters as are other sorts of professionals.

Exciting, vital teaching is teaching which is experimental, teaching which produces *new* knowledge for the teacher rather than simply applies old knowledge routinely or perfunctorily. This theme, implicit in much of the work of LAC proponents, finds explicit form in a book produced by the Talk Workshop Group (1982) at the Vauxhall Manor School in London. The teachers in this group met formally from 1974-1979 to study first writing across the curriculum at the school (1974-75) and then language across the curriculum (1975-79). Here is the way two participants described the "new" roles their group had to take on in order to pursue their studies of language and learning at the school.

> . . . because looking at language in schools is a critical study of our and the children's contemporary practice, we, the teachers, must become our own theoreticians, must become our own experts. Our theory, our "expertise," is in making sensitive inferences about an actual classroom experience, in noticing what is really going on. If the expert in the usual sense, who stands back from everyday reality of the classroom in order, ideally, to get a wider view of the scene, has a role in this process of discovery, it is simply to help the classroom teacher discover what is already there.

To become autonomous, creative, fully functioning professionals, then, teachers need to see themselves as theorizers *and* to become actually engaged in theorizing about, observing, and inquiring into the operations of their students and themselves. These two activities, theorizing and inquiring, are the key. From active theorizing comes an expanded and stronger basis for analyzing and for understanding what is actually going on in classrooms. From active inquiring comes a steady flow of new information which can be used to confirm or disconfirm the practical, working hypotheses which inevitably arise when theory-based analyses of classroom activity are regularly being conducted. When the theorizing and inquiring are "married in the lives of the people who do the job" of teaching children, they will not be abstract and irrelevant activities, but rather they will enhance and lend greater efficacy to the teaching practices which we all worry so much about.

When teachers become theorizers and inquirers as well as practitioners, when their role expands to include these truly intellectual activities as both central and valued, they will become more independent and "self-fashioning beings" (Diamond, 1982). For those administrators and others who want docile, submissive teachers, who fear a loss of their control to teachers who are more independent and self-fashioning, this agenda for teacher development is threatening. Inquiring, theorizing teachers *will* take more control over the entire range of their professional lives and duties, and power in schools will be redistributed as a result. That is inevitable, and it is the avenue to real, substantive, enduring reform in teaching and learning in our schools.

2

Language and Thinking

... by the invention of symbolic forms man has given
birth and lasting existence to thought.

Michael Polanyi, 1962

In Chapter 1, we took the position that learning, or the construction of knowledge, results from the symbolic transformation
of experience. Now, we want to qualify that position somewhat by
claiming that thought, or thinking, lies between experience and its
transformation through language to knowledge. A simple diagram
of this new position looks as follows:

experience ⟷ thought ⟷ language ⟷ knowledge

Each of us thinks about our experience unceasingly, when we
are awake or asleep. This thinking exists and occurs without language,
beneath language in effect. Thus, our thinking about experience is
both never-ending and nonlinguistic. The interesting question, then,
is: What happens to thought when we put it into words? How we
answer this question has important implications for our view of the
role of language in learning and the construction of knowledge and,
thus, for our view of how language should be used in classrooms.

What is the relationship between language and thinking in use?
For scholars and researchers, answering this question is difficult
enough. For teachers, with little time for scholarship, becoming
informed about language and thinking is even more difficult. Nevertheless, an understanding of this complex relationship is extremely
valuable for teachers of all ages of pupils and of all curricular subjects. Such an understanding illuminates teaching/learning processes
in fundamental ways, bringing increased efficacy to daily classroom
operations.

Language and Thinking Intertwined

Our intent is to present a perspective which may be useful as a starting point for teachers in attempting to understand more fully how language and thinking are related in use. This perspective consists of ten assumptions which we believe can be held with confidence. The assumptions, and the overall perspective which they provide, have proved useful to us both in thinking about language and thinking and in providing a rich source of practical implications for classroom teaching.

Few would disagree that thinking is an important goal of schooling. We can imagine few people who would consider thinking to be so unimportant for adult life as to give it low priority in school curricula. Most people want children to learn how to think, and most also see schools as a main sponsoring institution for that learning. In fact, what thinking is taken to mean or be is likely to be a matter of more widespread disagreement than whether its development through schooling is important or not.

The media provide some evidence of this disagreement. Recently, articles have appeared in newpapers and magazines, as well as in various educational publications, decrying the state of our students' thinking. Apparently, our students' abilities to engage in critical, analytical, or inferential thinking have declined along with their reading and writing abilities. Citing evidence from SAT scores, from findings of the National Assessment of Education Progress testing in writing, reading, and literature, and from reports made by individual colleges and researchers, these critics allege a thinking crisis. The '80s, they suggest, is the decade of concern for thinking, just as the '60s was for reading and the '70s for writing. In any event, thinking has become an important education issue.

Ostensibly, just as schools are maintained as places to teach thinking, they are maintained even more broadly as places for learning. The learning may result from explicit or implicit curricula, or both; it may be planned or incidental, lasting or short-lived, practical or impractical, abstract or concrete, intellectual or manual. No matter how cynical we may be about the potentialities and outcomes of schooling, we cannot deny that students do learn things in school. Nor can we deny that thinking of some sort is involved in that learning, whatever theory of thinking or learning we espouse. And all of this thinking and learning, regardless of how we view it, floats on a sea of talk, as Harold Rosen has so tellingly noted.

Schools are language-saturated institutions. They are places where books are thumbed, summarized and "revised," notes are dictated, made, kept and learnt, essays are prepared, written and marked, examination questions are composed and the attendant judgments made. Teachers explain, lecture, question, exhort, reprimand and make jokes. Pupils listen, reply, make observations, call out, mutter, whisper and make jokes. Small knots gather round over books, lathes, easels and retorts, or over nothing in classrooms, labs, workshops, craftrooms, corridors and toilets to chatter, discuss, argue, quarrel, plan, plot, teach each other, using words to stroke or strike. There are foundation-stones, notice-boards, blackboards, pin-up boards, circulars, full of injunctions, warnings, records of triumphs, mottoes, cuttings, compositions and graffiti. As the school day unfolds law and lore become established, puzzled over or rejected. (Barnes, Britton, and Rosen, 1969)

Schools sponsor many kinds of activities every day. In large part, those activities take place as or in or through language. Talking, listening, reading, and writing, in one combination or another, penetrate, even dominate, school life and activities, including manual, physical, and scientific areas of the curriculum. Language *use* is more totally, intimately, and irrevocably involved in school thinking and learning, of whatever kinds, than any other kind of activity. Even computers require "language" for their operation. Language, as much recent research suggests, plays a fundamental and powerful role in the conduct of school life and the shaping of school outcomes.

If school life and activities are extensively permeated and constituted by language, then the thinking that occurs and the learning that results must depend extensively on the *kinds* of language that are used (Parker, 1982a). This is the crux of our argument: if thinking and learning in schools are so extensively language related and language influenced, then teachers must understand what relationship language and thinking have. As we mentioned in Chapter 1, the initiators of LAC had little understanding of how the discussions which they sponsored in their classrooms led to thinking and learning. Because they lacked a perspective on the relation of language to thinking and learning, they were "flying blind" in their classrooms most of the time. Their students listened, talked, read, and wrote, and, ostensibly they thought and learned. Ostensibly, also, these linguistic activities contributed to the learning outcomes. Yet, these teachers couldn't explain how or why, which should be no great source of embarrassment, because psychologists and linguists can't either. Lacking a framework for developing such explanations, they could only stumble along, mostly requiring students to use language for *displaying* knowledge rather than for *constructing* it (Martin et al., 1976; Torbe and Medway, 1981; Medway, 1980).

All the "higher psychic functions" (or "higher psychological processes," as Vygotsky alternately called them) are functional systems consisting of less complex mental operations. People construct these systems to solve problems in the world, including the world of the mind. Language serves both as a means of organizing the system, often the primary means, and as a means of representing the system or its products symbolically. Concepts, of whatever sort in whatever field, are thus functional systems. People use them as an organized means, and organize them as a means, of thinking about some problem for the purpose of solving it. When we hear people talk or read what they write, we are witnessing at the same time a product of this functional process and a bit of the process in operation. Thus, it seems useful to view the symbolized concept not simply as a static product of thought but also as an evolving process of thinking. Seen from this perspective, concepts are "creative, not mechanical" or "ossified" formations, active parts of the "human intellectual process, constantly involved in serving communication, understanding, and problem solving" (Vygotsky, 1962).

Verbal thought generally, as with concepts, develops through use in specific life situations. Because all situations are social, verbal thought has a social basis and is steadily influenced in its development by the sociality of the contributory situations. To each situation the individual person brings her emerging powers and purposes, or what Dewey (1971) called the internal conditions of the individual. The individual has certain intentions or purposes she wants to realize and certain available means or powers to use in attempting their realization. For each person, the intentions and means are somewhat unique. At the same time, each situation has its unique features, what Dewey called the external conditions of the environment. In the event, each situation poses certain problems to be solved. What a person intends and what the situation poses as problems are mutually interactive and influential, though at times there may be considerable conflict between these two sets of conditions. What a person chooses to emphasize in a given situation from among her array of personal intentions depends somewhat on the objective features of the situation. But, by the same token, what she identifies from among these objective features as problems to be solved will in turn be shaped by her intentions.

In planning for classroom events or in responding to them as they unfold, teachers might best operate with these two sets of conditions clearly in mind, taking into account equally their learners' intentions and the objective features of the school environment that they have a hand in creating. Teaching would consist of organizing situations in the light of learners' intentions, and monitoring activities within them, as opposed to providing direct, didactic instruction offered with little or no concern for either set of conditions. This point was made tellingly by Martin et al. (1976), where the authors urged teachers to teach situations, not types of writing, particularly situations involving real audiences and, therefore, *genuine* communication and problem-solving.

If the situations organized by teachers pose problems which students indentify as calling for certain uses of language for their solution, then the verbal thinking which results will arise from the context and be directed toward solving the problems. The kinds of talking or writing students choose to do, in what sequence and in what relation to other sorts of manual or symbolic activities, would depend to an important extent on their emerging intentions, as well as on their prior experiences, knowledge, and interests. Each student individually, or as part of a group, would develop a functional system of mental and verbal activities to solve the problem.

Students talk and write better when their intentions are engaged and when they are doing the talking and the writing as part of a larger task or as a means of achieving a goal that includes more than simply talking or writing well. Writing to master the form leads to the isolation of writing and of thinking generally, from genuine intention to mechanism and ossification in thought and procedures: that is, to mindless, formulaic efforts. On the other hand, writing (or talking) from one's intentions to solve a self-defined if not self-chosen problem leads to vigorous and interesting writing (Martin, 1980).

Writing is one kind of verbal thinking; inner speaking, listening, speaking, and reading are others. All are, virtually simultaneously, both means and manifestation. For example, writing provides, on the one hand, a means for engaging in verbal thought and is, as such, a process. On the other hand, it represents or manifests the results of thinking, providing a record of its occurrence, and is, as such, a product. In both these aspects, writing (or any other use of language) can also be viewed as part of a functional system organized by the writer to solve a particular problem. In the event, the problem lies both in *and* beyond the writing, and the functional system typically incorporates both the writing and other activities, including other sorts of verbal thinking.

Seldom, in my experience, do teachers view pupils' use of language in this multifaceted way. Seldom do they view writing or any other use of language as both a *means of thinking* and a *manifestation of thought*. Most often, writing — or students' classroom contributions to the oral exchanges that are mistakenly called discussions — is taken as a product of thought so that it may be evaluated for its accuracy or completeness or logic. Seldom, also, is writing viewed as part of a functional system involving other activities functionally interlinked with the writing. Nearly always, the writing (or talking or reading) is viewed in isolation, both from other activities of the writer *and* from the writer's internal conditions. The writing is seldom seen as *for* anything, nor as a part of anything, nor as a process of doing or achieving anything other than mastering the form: essay, report, or story.

Historically, those investigating the relationship between language and thinking have taken one of three different positions. Some have viewed language and thinking as "identical," assuming that "thinking cannot occur without language" (Bolton, 1972). From this perspective, language determines the content, if not the structure, of thought (Adams, 1973). Others, taking an extreme opposite position, have regarded language and thinking as "entirely independent" of each other (Bolton, 1972). When viewed from this alternate perspective,

> language no longer serves as an explanatory principle. The structures of thought are seen to be derived from the child's actions. It is the child's activities that [first] constitute thinking. Language plays a supportive rather than a determining role in thinking. (Adams, 1973)

More recently, investigators have hypothesized a reciprocal or transactional relationship between the two. Language and thinking are seen neither as identical nor as totally separate. Rather, they are assumed to be distinct but intertwined, separate but mutually influential, activities linked by a process involving continual transactions between them. Proponents of this third position are concerned with verbal thought, thus admitting the independent existence of each while emphasizing their transaction and mutual influence.

The first position seems out of favor today. No one is using it as the basis for serious study of language/thinking relationships. Positions two and three, however, are being used and their relative merits actively debated. Though an oversimplification, it is fair to identify position two as a Piagetian position and three as a Vygotskyan one. We favor the Vygotskyan position, as the following ten points will illustrate.

The Origins of Language and Thinking

Both phylogenetically and ontogenetically, thought and language have different roots. That is, both arise from different sources in the developmental history of the individual and of the species.

Further, in their early developmental history, for individuals as well as for the species, thought and language developed along different lines, each independent of the other and with no clear-cut correlation between them. This initial assumption, drawn from discussions by Vygotsky (1962, 1978), is interesting on both counts. How, for example, must we think about the nature of thinking and its historical evolution for the species if we believe it to have arisen separately from language, with no interaction or mutual influence for some substantial period of time?

Such questions about the species, however, have more direct implications for linguists, psychologists, and anthropologists than for teachers. For how long do thought and language develop separately in individuals? When do they "meet"? What happens when that meeting occurs? Even after this meeting, do individuals continue to manifest forms of each which remain essentially "pure," uninfluenced by the other? The possible answers to these questions, proposed in light of this particular belief about the historical/developmental origins of thought and language, have direct implications for curriculum organization and teaching practices. If, for example, nonlinguistic kinds of thinking continue through life, as valid and useful forms of intellectual behavior, how might school curricula and classrooms best be organized to tap and develop these forms? This question, and its reverse about language, anticipate the second assumption.

Kinds of Language and Thought

This two-sided assumption, though it can be stated straightforwardly, has radical implications for our approaches to schooling. On the one hand, early speech is nonintellectual. It is neither influenced in its course of development by thinking, nor does it express thought or serve as a means of thinking. Functionally, early language is expressive and social rather than intellectual. It serves to express emotional responses to experience and to create and preserve social relationships through communication, both pre-speech and post-speech. Because nonintellectual forms of speech continue throughout life, serving important expressive and social purposes for older people as they do for younger, teachers ought to respond in their organization of curricula and classrooms, though by and large they have not.

On the other hand, three kinds of thought can be assumed to exist: prelinguistic, linguistic, and nonlinguistic. The first is thought-in-action: thought which involves the development of increasingly coordinated schemes of action by children for the accomplishment of various purposes. Piaget, preeminently, has described this kind of thinking, which proceeds in its developmental course without the intervention or incorporation of symbol use. Because we now have strong evidence that children do think before they develop language, it is no longer possible to believe, in general, that the course of intellectual development commences with the onset of speech, nor is it thus possible to believe in particular that this course of development can be influenced totally through language, especially through language exercises in schools. This kind of assumption, still held by many educators, seems irrational today.

Linguistic (or verbal) thought, which represents one manifestation of the broader category of symbolic thought, results from the intersection of thought and language (see below). It is thought influenced and directed, both in use and in development, by language. This particular kind of thought occupies the dominant place in American schools, to the extent that many educators assume it to be the only kind of thought.

Finally, there is nonlinguistic thought, thought engaged in by individuals *after* the onset of language which is influenced neither in use nor in development by language. At this point, we see nonlinguistic thought as including both advanced forms of thought-in-action and thought carried on through other symbolic media like dance, mime, painting, or sculpture. Again, American educators, by equating thought with language, have further rationalized their allocation of physical and artistic activities to the farthest periphery of the curriculum. If one assumes that thought is not involved in physical and artistic creativity, then it is easy to value these activities little and thus to neglect them almost totally in formulating curriculum policy. If, on the other hand, one assumes the constant presence of thought, both linguistic and nonlinguistic, and therefore the necessity of supporting both kinds in use and in development, then a curriculum policy must follow which gives physical and artistic activity a more central status.

The Intersection of Thought and Language

At about age two, as Vygotsky (1962, 1978) has eloquently argued, thought and language intersect in the life of the child. Before this point, child thought has been essentially nonverbal. Now it becomes essentially verbal. That is, verbal thought becomes the major form of thought. Before this point, child speech has been essentially nonrational. Now, influenced by its intersection with thought, language becomes essentially rational, though not exclusively so.

Also at this moment of intersection, the "nature of development itself changes." Not only are thought and speech transformed by this intersection, but the entire course of psychological development is transformed from being primarily biologically determined to being primarily sociohistorically determined. Obviously, schooling is a major factor in the sociohistorical process experienced by children and is therefore a determining force in the course of each child's development. How this force is constructed and applied, we assume, must make a difference in the way it shapes and directs each child's development. How, then, can curricula and classrooms be managed, given the transformations of thought and language which have already occurred in children's development, so as to play the most beneficial role possible in their further learning and development? Just asking the question in these terms, radically new for many educators, implies a need for sweeping revision of many school programs.

The Outcome of Egocentric Speech

In his account of speech development, Vygotsky portrays speech as having social origins. Children, he argues, develop speech as a means of conducting social communications and of creating and participating in social relationships. Egocentric speech develops from social speech, as a later form, rather than the other way round. It develops as a first and initially crude means of planning and organizing the self and the environment for carrying out actions. In effect, it operates as an accompaniment to action, but one that influences the nature and conduct of action.

In this way, egocentric speech forms the "bridge" between social and inner speech. When, at about age five, egocentric speech begins to disappear as an external form of behavior, rather than vanishing entirely as Piaget hypothesized, it goes "underground" and is reconstructed internally by the individual as inner speech. As inner speech, it then serves as the primary means of private, verbal thinking and makes possible, on the internal psychological plane, actions which had been possible only on the external plane as physical action. That is, children can now "act" mentally on imagined objects instead of being limited to acting physically on actual objects, organizing their actions in advance and gathering resources which are not immediately visible. Vygotsky not only proposed a view opposed to Piaget's on this issue, but further saw this internalization of egocentric speech as the crucial second stage in the now sociohistorically governed process of psychological development.

The Social Basis of Intellectual Development

Like both communicative and linguistic development, intellectual development has its basis in social behavior and occurs through the means of social interaction. Mead (1934) explained this process by proposing the concept of the generalized other. In his account, mind grows through the incorporation of others' viewpoints into our own thought processes. He meant, quite literally, that we reconstruct our thinking about aspects of the world in the light of our grasp of how others think. Gradually, we develop a concept of the "generalized other": how other people *in general* think about whatever it is that we are thinking about. This gradual development occurs as we encounter others' viewpoints through social interaction. Hence, no social interaction with others who offer us an expanded range of alternative viewpoints, no new viewpoints to incorporate into our thinking, no intellectual development.

Vygotsky offered a similar perspective, asserting the dual occurrence of the higher psychological processes, first on the *interpersonal* level as a *social process* and then on the *intrapersonal* level as an internal reconstruction of this social process. His own description is difficult to improve upon:

> Every function in the child's cultural development appears twice: first, on the social level, and later, on the individual level; first, between people (interpsychological), and then inside the child (intrapsychological). This applies equally to voluntary attention, to logical memory, and to the formation of concepts. All the higher functions originate as actual relations between human individuals. (Vygotsky, 1978)

What do these five "background" assumptions add up to, and what purpose do they serve? Taken together, these initial assumptions produce the following theoretical picture. Thought and language arise from different sources and, until about age two, follow different developmental paths. Before these paths cross, children's speech is nonintellectual and their thought, nonverbal. When these paths do cross, each form of behavior is radically and permanently transformed, as is the entire course of psychological development from that moment forward. Biology loses dominance over the developmental process as society gains it. Slightly later, starting about age five, the egocentric speech which had developed as an offshoot of social speech begins to disappear, going underground to form inner speech. From this point on inner speech constitutes our primary means of verbal thinking. This thinking, this verbal process in our heads, represents an inner reconstruction, on a psychological plane, of prior behavior enacted on an outer, social plane. In fact, all psychological development represents this two-stage process: movement from outwardly constructed social transactions to inwardly reconstructed psychological operations.

For us, these five points provide a substantive, principled position which gives direction and coherence to our thinking. The next five points follow as implications of this initial position.

Advantages of Verbal Thought

Verbal thought frees us from the structure and objects of the immediate concrete, visual situation. Through the means of verbal thought our field of action is expanded. We can "see" things in our minds, and thus we are no longer tied in our thinking to the objects displayed before us. We can literally imagine objects that are not there which we might want to use in problem-solving, just as we can imagine sequences of actions which we have not yet taken.

This increased flexibility in problem-solving which verbal thinking brings includes other important gains as well. We can analyze past events and plan future actions, as well as locate, use, or store resources that we might anticipate wanting or needing. Importantly, verbal thinking allows us to represent events symbolically (to ourselves and to others) and thus to anticipate and predict the future. This process of constructing a representation of the world for use as a source of anticipatory hypotheses about events, plus the possible reconstruction of it in the light of the events themselves, George Kelly (1963) saw as our most fundamentally human activity.

Vygotsky (1962) took a somewhat different tack, viewing the possibilities of verbal thinking for the *self*-regulation of behavior, including mental behavior, as its most important contribution to human development and functioning. Because signs have an inward orientation, as opposed to the external orientation of tools, verbal thinking allows us "to overcome impulsive action" and "to master [our] own behavior."

Interaction of Language and Thinking

It is in the arena of the self-regulatory potential of verbal thinking that our next point is located. Because verbal thinking permits thought to be turned inward, toward the self, it permits thought to become recursive — to make itself its own object.

> Language permits thought to fold back upon itself; the product of thought itself becomes an object that thought can operate upon. (Smith, 1982)

In this recursive process, language and thought not only interact but also are mutually influential. The "language that our thought produces modifies our thought as it is produced" (Smith, 1982). Smith says "modifies"; we say *transforms*. In our view, language transforms thought (and vice versa). That is, as language "freezes time," capturing bits of the "ongoing and undifferentiated" flow of our thinking and making those bits manifest, the thinking thus captured and expressed is transformed by the language which makes this process possible. We never know the exact nature of underlying nonlinguistic thinking because the linguistic version that we hear or see reflects a transformation of it.

This process, this "continual movement back and forth" between thought and word, is important because language, used to express thought, "gives thought something different to consider" (Smith, 1982). Thought can think about itself. Thus, the recursive potential of verbal thinking also makes possible its reflexive potential. We can isolate some of our mental behaviors from our total mental activity, enabling us

> to focus on this process and to enter into a new relationship with it. In this way becoming conscious of our operations and viewing each as a process of a certain kind, such as remembering or imagining, leads to their mastery. (Vygotsky, 1962)

By understanding our thinking processes, as such understanding is made possible by verbal thinking, we can master them. This mastery of the processes of our own thinking, we believe, provides the best pathway for the development of the higher psychological processes in general, and writing provides a unique means for developing this reflexive control of our knowledge.

The Development of Analytic Competence

As we grow older, we tend to use language more frequently in ways that involve greater "context-free elaboration" (Bruner, 1975). In most ordinary situations, our verbal thinking represents little more than "a quick compilation" of words expressing a response to fairly immediate events. Occasionally, however, we engage in a more deliberate serial ordering or reordering of events which includes conscious choice among alternatives "not present to attention." These alternatives take the form of propositions, and their serial odering entails a logical activity which carries with it the possibility of extrapolating the implications of these propositions to their logical extreme. That is, we can work from the initial propositional alternatives to their ultimate, logical conclusions, leaving real events or facts behind.

The propositions in this network, because they are connected logically rather than empirically, represent the development of analytic competence, a step beyond either linguistic or communicative competence. This new, language-dependent competence involves the prolonged operation of thought processes exclusively on linguistic representations, on propositional structures, accompanied by strategies of thought and problem-solving appropriate not to direct experience with objects and events but with ensembles of propositions. It is heavily metalinguistic in nature . . . and it is strikingly the case that, more often than not, it generates new notational systems like mathematics, or more powerfully elaborated forms of the natural language like poetry. It is studied little. (Bruner, 1975)

Once we have created a symbol to stand for a concept, "it becomes possible to explore its presuppositional structure, [and] to compile the procedures related to it." This exploration of the presuppositional structure of our symbols does not happen automatically. We do not ordinarily engage in this kind of verbal thinking, which requires "more ordered operations on a set of formal categories" than is common in our everyday "functional processing of events," because doing so

[reverses] the direction of thinking between *reality* and *possibility*. . . . Possibility no longer appears merely as an extension of an empirical situation or of actions actually performed. Instead it is reality that is now secondary to possibility. (Piaget and Inhelder, 1969).

The Construction of Imaginary Worlds

Language (and other symbol systems) enables thought to create new worlds of imagination and fantasy. Verbal thinking enables us to do more than create a representation or theory of the world in our head to serve us in anticipating, negotiating, and interpreting the practical realities of living. It enables us also to create alternative worlds, places "where we can explore ideas, generate fantasies, experience wishes, hopes and fears, and plan all our activities" (Smith, 1982).

Susanne Langer (1978) called this kind of thinking "presentational" to distinguish it from "discursive thinking," which accords with "analytic competence." Each kind of thinking, presentational as well as discursive, has its own distinct characteristics and logic, though the structure of presentational logic has not yet been adequately analyzed. In general, though, discursive thinking can be viewed as linear, analytic, sequential, and presentational thinking as associative, holistic, simultaneous. Thus, language enables thought to develop in two general and different directions: toward analytic or fictional competence, toward realistic or imaginative syntheses, toward science or art.

Unfortunately, American educators have, with few exceptions, committed themselves to the development only of analytic/discursive thinking, neglecting imaginative/presentational thinking almost completely. The source of this problem lies in the lack of a perspective on the relationship of language and thinking which asserts *clearly* the existence of imaginative/presentational thinking as a true alternative mode of thought, complete with its own logic and potentialities. Thus, we can make claims about the value of the arts in education, or of the role of imagination in science, but no one will take these claims seriously who does not already believe in the existence of a separate and distinct kind of thinking which has equal status and value in psychological development, scientific discovery, and social progress.

The Label: Evolutionary Instrumentalism

Throughout this discussion, we have emphasized the interaction and mutual influence of language and thinking as well as the potentialities of human functioning which this mutually influential interaction creates. Language, by making thought manifest, enables it to become both recursive and reflexive, while thought, on the other hand, enables language to develop in two general and different directions: toward both analytic and imaginative competence. It seems reasonable, then, to view this relationship overall as an instrumental one: language serves generally and variously as an instrument of thought, which is to say language serves as a means of making thought manifest and of transforming it. The relationship also seems to be evolutionary in the sense that it is always evolving, always taking on new functions or playing new roles in new situations. It is never static.

Vygotsky described the higher psychological processes as functional systems of lower or less complex psychological processes. Individuals create these functional systems in specific social situations to solve specific problems, and it is in precisely this sense that these systems of psychological processes are functional. Since no two situations are quite the same, nor do they pose exactly similar problems for our solution, no two higher psychological processes are quite the same, nor do language or thought play quite the same role in either process. Thus, the role of language in both the formation and representation of such systems can be seen as constantly evolving and changing.

Classroom Implications of This Perspective

In its most productive forms, teaching requires teachers to understand and take into account two broad sets of conditions in their daily operations. One set is under their control; the other is not. These are, respectively, the outer conditions of the environment and the inner conditions of pupils. By the former, Dewey meant all those external aspects of schools, classrooms, curricula, teaching techniques, and teacher values which lie outside pupils' psychological lives and processes and which teachers can arrange for physically and intellectually. Because control over these outer conditions lies, more or less, in the hands of teachers, they constitute the proper domain of pedagogical discussion and activity.

By the latter, the inner conditions of individuals, Dewey meant the psychological processes of pupils: their inner mental states and operations, including their psychosocial history. These processes he called the "powers and purposes of the child": what children *can* do and what they *want* to do. Though teachers must make every effort to understand these inner conditions and to take them into account in arranging the outer conditions, they cannot be controlled in the same way. Pupils' inner conditions are a given, though of equal importance in affecting the success of the entire teaching/learning enterprise.

In effect, we have presented a perspective which is useful for understanding one aspect of the inner conditions of pupils: their ongoing, and developing, processes of verbal thinking as these processes both reveal their powers and purposes and permit their realization and development. So the primary implication of this perspective for teaching lies in its potential for understanding that set of conditions which, while not directly under the control of teachers, is crucial to all learning.

This perspective, though, also has important secondary implications for the ways in which teachers arrange the outer conditions of the environment. The following five implications are drawn from our teaching and from the work of teachers who are implementing a similar perspective on language and thinking. Each implication is stated somewhat generally, and our purpose is to provide starting points for teachers to use in working out the techniques most suitable to the powers and purposes of their pupils.

1. *If language and thinking interact in mutually influential and transformational ways, then different kinds of language use in different situations make possible the expression and transformation of different kinds of thinking.* It is important, therefore, for teachers

to arrange for, and to support a wide range of uses of language in classrooms so that students may undertake a wide variety of kinds of verbal thinking. We find it most useful to think of this variety of language *use* as having two important dimensions. The first dimension ranges from informal to formal, and the second, from analytic to imaginative:

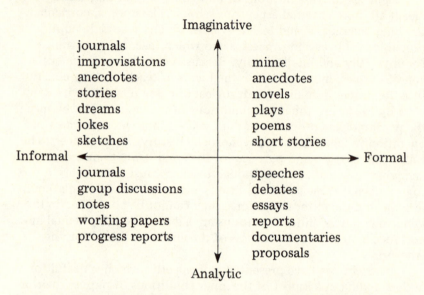

Informal uses of language are particularly important for the early stages of understanding new information and new ideas. Faced with puzzling, difficult, or upsetting experiences or material, we typically turn to our most familiar kinds of language to begin the process of understanding and/or coming to terms with them. Often, imaginative and analytic kinds of verbal thinking are mixed together at the beginning, and necessarily so, as we untangle the emotional import and construct the intellectual meaning of these experiences. As experiences, information, concepts (or whatever) are more fully grasped, it becomes appropriate then to communicate our understanding in more public, conventional forms of discourse.

These may take analytic/transactional forms, or they may take imaginative/poetic forms. The former is most valuable for drawing out the logical implications of an understanding of something, and the latter is most valuable for evaluating the understanding in the light of our deepest personal values.

To sum up: for an optimal development and expression of understanding to take place, a full spectrum of types of language use for thinking must be envisioned, planned for, and acknowledged as valid. The spectrum includes informal and formal uses, as well as imaginative and analytic ones. Only when such a full spectrum is implemented in substantial ways will teachers be fully supporting a wide range of verbal thinking in use and in development.

2. *From this perspective, all four uses of language are integrated in normal living and in development.* Therefore, both curricula and teaching techniques should assume and support such integration. Speaking, for example, should not be isolated and taught as a separate curricular "subject," nor should writing or reading. As children's powers and purposes are brought into conjunction with the curriculum, listening, speaking, writing, and reading should flow into and out of one another seamlessly, without compartmentalization. Language, in all its uses, is an instrument of thinking; this function is especially crucial at those moments when children encounter the events of the curriculum in ways that fully engage their powers and purposes.

When we plan and teach our courses, we want students to listen, talk, write, and read and to improve at each. Neither, however, is a primary goal of our teaching. Our primary goal is to engage students in thinking about the problems posed for them by the curriculum. To do this thinking most fully and productively, they will need to use language in all four modes, and the shifts from use to use and the combinations of uses will be most productive when they flow from one to the other naturally in relation to the progress in understanding which is being made. That is, whether students are writing informally in their journals, discussing material spontaneously, reading and discussing a draft of a paper, listening to a lecture, reading a text, or formulating questions that they want to have answered will depend on the relation between their emerging understanding and the kinds of verbal thinking which will help them most to move forward with their understanding.

We seldom teach them directly to write or read (or talk or listen). Rather we assist them in using language more powerfully as a means of thinking and learning. That is, we assist them in developing functional systems of verbal thought which include informal and formal *and* imaginative and analytic uses of listening, talking, writing, and reading to solve various learning problems. When the "seamless flow" is going, they are literally and simultaneously using language for thinking and learning, learning how to do this on their own, and developing a theory of how this process occurs. They are learning and theorizing about learning at the same time, and in this process, they develop as both users of language and as thinkers (Wells et al., 1981).

3. *As individuals use language of various sorts for thinking and learning purposes, considerable struggle may occur.* The effort to understand, to come to terms with or to construct knowledge about experience, especially abstract school material, may be difficult or even painful. And "errors" will be made along the way. We have learned, though, and not without difficulty, to stand back and let the struggle take place. For the process of struggling, which includes the making and self-correcting of errors, lies at the heart of learning. If, as teachers, we offer corrections, procedures, formulations, or answers too soon, students will not use language fully in the construction of their own knowledge. Such assistance, when we do offer it or another student does, must be given judiciously at just those points where individuals or groups truly need assistance in order to move on.

These efforts by students to construct knowledge through language embedded in social interaction provide the interpersonal occurrences of what they will later reconstruct internally as intrapersonal psychological processes (see #5 below). Thus, the struggle to understand, with verbal thinking as the primary means, must be arranged for and supported through a shifting but coherent variety of social interactions and uses of language. The coherence will be psychological not logical: it will come from the ways in which pupils face and solve the learning problems posed by the curriculum, and not from the logical organization of the curriculum. The nature of this coherence can be understood and anticipated generally, but it cannot be preplanned in any complete, programmatic way. Predetermined lessons, particularly those with a tight logical structure, will considerably impede, if not eliminate, the full potentialities of verbal thought for learning.

4. *If we distinguish between the construction of knowledge and its communication, or between the process of learning and the display of results from that process, it becomes clear that both deserve full support in classrooms.* That is, verbal thinking for learning and for communicating about that learning needs to be planned for and supported. In practical terms, this means providing opportunities for work that is evaluated and work that is not. As research by Douglas Barnes (1976), Barnes and Todd (1977), Martin et al. (1976), Torbe and Medway (1981) and others suggests, the teacher's intent to evaluate students' work nearly always causes them to stop struggling *to understand* curriculum material and to start struggling *to find correct answers*, whether they understand those answers or not. What becomes important for students is to give answers that teachers deem correct, and they put aside any intent to comprehend or make

meaning. It is fair to say that evaluation *of any kind* deflects students *from* using language to think and learn *to* using language to get right answers. Sometimes, as Barnes and Todd (1977) have documented, the mere presence of the teacher in a discussion group causes this deflection, regardless of any evaluative intent. Students apparently see teachers as evaluators, thus assuming such a role even when it has been temporarily put aside. Teachers may have to work hard, as we certainly have to with each new group of students, to convince them that sometimes we have no evaluative intent, that sometimes our sole intent is to witness and assist with their learning.

5. *Finally, as the last and most important implication of this perspective, we see the provision of opportunities for students to reflect on their own processes of thinking and learning.* Ultimately, understanding how we think and learn gives us a control over these psychological processes which comes in no other way than through reflective thinking. This means, in effect, making our higher psychological processes, the functional systems of subprocesses that we construct to solve complex conceptual problems, the object of verbal thought. Or, to put it slightly differently, it means constructing functional systems to solve the problem of understanding the sources, structures, functions, and implications of our functional systems. Since these functional systems are psychological, since they happen in the brain where they cannot be observed, they can only be understood theoretically. So, when we refer to reflective thinking, we are advocating the involvement of students of all ages in constructing theories of their own thinking and learning processes, which is their means of gaining reflective control over these processes, and thus, over their knowledge.

From young ages, students can engage in this process quite beneficially as long as they are able to use the kinds of language which are most familiar and most instrumental for them in doing this kind of verbal thinking. At least from six or seven onward, children can think about how they do and learn mathematics or reading or writing, how they learn by discussing things in groups, how they learn sports or music, or how they solve problems on microcomputers. Usually, as the Rosens (1973) discovered in their visits to British primary schools, the language of such thinking is informal, spontaneous, personal, and idiosyncratic. They found that the best kinds of thinking appeared in those pieces of children's writing that were relatively undifferentiated formally. That is, the best thought occurred in pieces which least resembled essays or reports or stories as adults think of them.

Though we may think of theorizing as a formidable, formal, or artificial activity, in our experience most people want to know how things work, including their own minds. Such theorizing is quite natural, and naturally interesting, when it is being done about the self (or close friends or family) and when it is not posed as a set task with formal rules and requirements for its undertaking. Talking in pairs or in small, informally structured groups, writing in journals or in other free-writing forms, younger children can reflect on and discuss with others their own higher psychological processes. For older students, such reflective thought can, gradually and carefully, be made the *topic* of reading, discussion, and writing.

In graduate courses for teachers, we require a class journal in which they write three to four entries per week in response to any aspect of the course which is of interest or concern. We ask that one entry per week be devoted to a discussion of how they have used language to learn something related to the course. At the end of the course, we ask them to select four or five such entries which they find interesting or illuminating and to write a brief, informal paper in which they explain what they think they have learned about thinking and learning from this process. Then, we discuss their "findings," and they have an opportunity to modify their summaries if they wish. We do not evaluate these collections; they are for their learning and ours only.

In appropriately modified ways, such a procedure can be instituted with pupils from about age seven upward. If pupils involved themselves in such reflective verbal thinking informally from, say, age seven to fifteen and more formally from about fifteen on, their growth of mind through the development of reflective control of their knowledge would, we predict, be extraordinary. In effect, they would have been doing cognitive/developmental psychology for much of their lives, and so they would be practicing psychologists of a sort, sophisticated about the kinds of questions, issues, and problems considered within this discipline.

3

Writing and the Construction of Knowledge

Writing can be transformational. Through writing we can transform our experience symbolically, creating new ways of seeing it, new meanings for it, and new relationships to it. We can, quite literally, *know* the world differently through the transformations of our experience that we make through writing. Poets and journal-keepers have testified amply to this power of writing, as have scientists.

Through writing we can also transform ourselves. We can come *to know* ourselves differently and, thus, *to be* different in the world. We can, for example, construct a new self in writing, which we may then enact experimentally in our lives (see George Kelly's work (1955) with fixed-role therapy and C. T. P. Diamond's work (1983) with teachers). In many of the National Writing Project summer institutes, participants have experienced self-transformation through the twin processes of writing and discussing that writing with involved and supportive peers (Parker, 1982b). And not only can we transform our experience and ourselves through our writing, we can transform others' views of us. Through hearing or reading our work, others may reconstruct, perhaps radically, who they think we are.

To make this claim more concrete, here are two pieces of writing which transformed the teachers' views of the students who wrote them. The pieces may also have been transformational for the writers, though we don't know that. The first piece was written by a ninth-grade boy, one of three mainstreamed students in a bottom-level English class and perhaps the most severely handicapped student in this high school.

Things That Are Green

Green is grass, frogs, the box of Fuji film with red, and trees. It reminds me of Green Bay, Wisconsin. Green smells like limes.

Green is also the color of bushes and pine trees. The signs of a freeway are green. Green is the color of the New York Jets football team. Green is the color of football fields.

The second piece was written by a twelfth-grade boy in the same school, also in the bottom ability level. This boy was not handicapped, just deeply disaffected with school and considered by his teachers to be a very weak student. He wrote this piece in a 40-minute class period.

The expectations rise with the morning sun. The cold January air bites at every part of your body and you wonder what force drives you to be here.

All grows silent and eerie as you wait for the first sighting. And then, as if out of nowhere, three huge Mallards soar in from the right. With their wings cupped, they glide into our sneakily set decoys, as silently as the winter morning.

Suddenly, as if on cue, we jump up and open fire. The first shots just seem to get their attention, and they begin to fly upward, in a panic. The second shots seem to do little more than the first. But by now everybody has lined up their shot, and it is your last shot, so you squeeze slowly on the trigger. It seems to take hours for it to finally fire. When it finally does, and you see your bird fold up and fall towards the earth, you know why you came.

Both teachers were amazed and delighted with these pieces. Neither had thought her student capable of producing such lovely writing. Reading the pieces of writing transformed each teacher's view of her student, not only as a writer but also as a student and person. The pieces created a new, more positive regard by the teacher for the students, and that change in perspective was permanent.

This is the background: our belief in the transformational possibilities of writing. Obviously, much of the writing people do every day is not transformational for them. Much of it is routine and is perfunctorily, if not mechanically, done. People write lists, notes, letters, orders, memos, minutes, reports, proposals, evaluations, etc. without transforming their experience or themselves in any way. Nonetheless, the potential for transformation is always there waiting to be taken up.

Against the background of our belief in this possibility, this potentiality, of writing, we present our discussion of the role of writing in the learning process, the foreground of this chapter. This discussion includes some examples of students' writing which seem to have played an important role in their learning.

Learning

Learning is continuous, always in process. Like the mind itself, it is always becoming and never being, always forming and never formed. Our brain transacts unceasingly with the world, and learning results, just as unceasingly. This process of transacting and learning has no beginnings or endings, no fixed points of stopping or starting, just as the world happening has no beginnings or endings. Moreover, the world does not double back upon itself. Events, with their beginnings and endings, are human constructions, products of our consciousness. We create events by segmenting the ceaseless, unduplicated happening of the world, giving the segments labels of our creation.

We do this to make sense of our experience. By labeling events as Type A or Type B, we are able to identify patterns in the constant flow. Thus, we give ourselves a retrospect and a prospect, a history and a future. We also give ourselves a means to bring these constructed events within the realm of our prediction and control.

From this transactionalist-constructivist perspective, learning is a constructed event. The world happens as it happens, and people do as they do. Some of these happenings we call language and others, learning. If this event of Type A is language and that event of Type B is learning, and we construe them as co-occurring in some meaningful way, then ostensibly we can arrange for their regular, predictable, and controlled occurrence.

So what's in these names we give to reality as we experience it happening? To some extent, everything. What we see when we look for learning, or for anything else, in the flow of reality is determined by what we take learning to be. Often, what we take something to be is captured by the label we give it.

One researcher took as the starting point for her study a teacher's insistence that her "lower track students did not write." The teacher considered this a major source of frustration in her teaching. The researcher, however, found the classroom to be a beehive of writing activity. Students wrote notes to each other and reminders to themselves, designed word games, drew up contracts, and made lists. When the researcher discussed these observations with the teacher, she initially dismissed it with, "Oh, I don't consider that to be writing."

That the teacher chose to count some behaviors as writing, while excluding others which appeared similar, is not surprising. Her "definition" of writing, shared by many educators and parents, kept her from categorizing certain student behaviors as writing. Another observer, using a different definition of writing, saw different events in that teacher's classroom. A major goal of ethnography is to describe the frameworks or definitions used by members of a culture, and thus to explain how certain people see the world and why (Smith, 1982).

We see (or experience) reality only indirectly, through the lens provided by those labels we use to segment its flow. When we change labels, we change what we see as events. At best, through our construings and reconstruings, we create more viable labels, ones which help us achieve our goals more successfully.

Learning, apparently, is an especially difficult set of events to detect. (Language is much easier to agree on.) Certainly, we argue about the label and its meaning a good deal, and typically we settle for a *post hoc* determination of its occurrence. Seldom do we confront the special difficulties involved in attempting to observe learning *in progress.* As a result, we have few tools for catching learning on the wing, so to speak: for glimpsing its contours and directions in the activities of our students' ongoing classroom lives.

To do this, we must operate like skilled bird watchers. Like them, we must know what we are looking at, learning, and not something else, and we must be patient. Knowing what learning is means having a theory of learning in our heads, a learning-watchers guidebook if you will. Otherwise we may miss our target altogether, or not know it when we see it. We also need to be in the right place at the right time and to be alert, attentive observers. The right place is the learner's habitat, the place where her purposes and powers are in full play and where she is most fully engaged in the spontaneous researches which lie at the center of her construction of knowledge. Such attentive observation requires a steady and clear focus on what she is doing, an open-eyed witnessing of her activities within the framework of her experience and her view of the world. Quite obviously, standing in front of the classroom focusing on teaching in order to enact a preplanned agenda violates all these conditions. The front of the classroom is the teacher's habitat, not the learner's, and the purposes of the preplanned lesson are the teacher's, not hers. And the theory in use is about teaching, not learning.

This chapter is primarily about learning, and only secondarily about teaching. When we discuss teaching, it is to describe what teachers might do to support and assist students in learning, with special concern for the role writing can play in that process. The talk about teaching is ancillary to talk about learning, and that is our initial message. To assist students in using language as an instrument of learning, teachers must shift their attention from teaching to learning, from a concern with their purposes and activities to students' purposes and the activities which they might undertake to achieve them. Teachers cannot make learning appear any more than the bird watcher can make a bird appear, though both can arrange the conditions somewhat. Beyond this arrangement of conditions, all either can do is wait, take what comes, and make the most intelligent possible response to it.

This point is crucial for teacher education. The more skillfully teachers can arrange the classroom conditions for learning and the more intelligently they can respond to learning in progress, the more successful will their (and the school's) instructional programs be. Such intelligent and deliberate response is a deep act of mind requiring psychological, sociological, linguistic and pedagogical knowledge, as well as a commitment to students as human beings.

Clearly then, what any teacher thinks learning looks like is crucial to her observations as well as to her other teacherly operations. We cannot tell you what "it" is. We can only give you our current construction, which is all that learning theorists can do either. They can only tell you what, in general or in theory, they take learning to be and, based on that construction, what they see when they look for it in reality.

Our theory of learning has three major features which have proved helpful in catching learning on the wing. These three features of our learning theory are not to be taken as hypotheses to be tested against the writing and found to be true or not. Nor are they qualities to be looked for *in the writing*. Rather, they are aspects of a perspective: a place to see *from*, *to* the writing. We believe them to be true, so for us their truth is not at issue. We are also passionately committed to them, in Polanyi's sense (1962), so that is not at issue either. What is at issue, first, is how we use them and how they work. Beyond that is the issue of how illuminating it may be for you to look briefly at some bits of the world through this same lens. If you operate as if our theory were true, the experience you have may result simply in confirming your present theory; it may, though, result in your reconstructing your present theory in the direction of ours.

To repeat: we construct knowledge through our transactions with objects, people, symbol systems, ideas, values. That process constitutes learning. Three features of this process have proved crucial in our formation of a useful working model.

1. Learning has a social basis and involves the reconstruction of social processes as individual psychological processes.
2. Learning has a "from-to" structure.
3. Learning requires that new experience or information be *used* in order to be constructed as knowledge.

We learn through the internal reconstruction of external operations. This process of "internalization" consists of a series of transformations, two of which are relevant here. First, "an operation that initially represents an external activity is reconstructed and begins to occur internally." We *do* something physically, and then we reconstruct the process of that action in our mind as a psychological or thinking process (Calkins, 1983, for a description of Susie's writing development). As a result, we can do "it," whatever that is, in our mind without having to otherwise do "it" in the world. From this perspective, thought is internalized action.

In the give and take of social interaction, with its verbal and nonverbal aspects, we engage in those intellectual operations which constitute thinking. Together with other people, we qualify, clarify, amend, judge, justify, analyze, synthesize, generalize, speculate, theorize, and evaluate, to name some labels given to kinds of thinking. Our participation in these operations socially, *inter*personally, enables us to reconstruct them individually, *intra*personally, and carry them out alone in our minds. Thus, when we watch the verbal transactions of small groups and study transcripts of them (Barnes and Todd, 1977), we are witnessing those social processes which children will subsequently reconstruct internally *as individual thinking processes.* Therefore, the kinds and qualities of these social processes, including particularly the uses of talking, directly shape the kinds and qualities of thinking that result. It would seem that, if children do not participate in exploring, hypothesizing, speculating, generalizing, or theorizing as part of the process of their social experience and interaction, in schools or elsewhere, they may not develop the ability to do these kinds of thinking on their own.

The second notion, that learning has a "from-to" structure, we have borrowed from Michael Polanyi (1962, 1968). In any act of knowing, Polanyi claims, "we *attend from* something for attending *to* something else." We attend from what we already know, what has been internalized, to the thing we are concerned with doing. Meaning, displaced away from us, lies in the task or problem we are attending to: in "the comprehensive activity in which we are primarily interested." We are thus focally aware of this comprehensive activity and subsidiarily aware of the knowledge we are coming from, or using, to accomplish this activity. If we shift our focal attention to what we are coming from, the elementary acts which make up our performance, our performance breaks down because it loses its purpose and its meaning.

Polanyi's classic example is of bicycle riding. When we ride a bicycle, he claims, we are focally aware of the comprehensive activity of riding, including where we are going and what is happening around us. We are only subsidiarily aware of *how* we are achieving this performance: of what we are doing with our body and hands, and what actual principle of balance we are operating. If our awareness were shifted to an analysis of this principle of balance, we would fall off the bicycle.

More familiar to us would be the act of writing. When we do a piece of writing, we are focally aware of the "meaning" or "artifact" we are attempting to create. We are, thus, attending *from* what we know about language and the conventions of written discourse, among other things, *to* the whole piece we are making. If we focus on the means, whether it be grammatical knowledge or knowledge of writing conventions, our performance breaks down. We lose our sense of purpose and meaning in the focus on meaningless details. Peter Elbow (1976) calls this "premature editing," and we know its effects are true for us as well as for the less skilled writers we teach.

The third notion comes mainly from a brief manifesto written by Piaget (1975). Understanding or knowing anything, he claims, occurs when we actually use that something to invent or make something else. Given facts to be learned, we construct knowledge from those facts by making them the means of doing something else rather than the end of the doing: the instrument for achieving another goal rather than the goal itself. Especially when the new goal is ours, when we are inventing something which reflects our intentions and not someone else's, the facts are reconstructed, and thus known, most fully and permanently.

Writing and Learning: Examples

Some teachers are willing to experiment with new ways of assisting students in using language, particularly writing, for learning. Such experiments, though, can be threatening, for they involve both teachers and students in adopting new perspectives and in taking on new roles in the classroom. Teachers must shift their attention somewhat, or even considerably, from their *teaching* operations and activities to their students' *learning* operations and activities. Such experiments require teachers to decenter and to take on a new observer/ assister role which may bring feelings of loss of control and authority. Put simply, teachers must place students at center stage of classroom learning.

Because learning is located in, and flows from, the activities of students, at best teachers can arrange classroom conditions, working alongside students to support, assist, and direct the activities through which they construct their knowledge of the curriculum content. This emphasis of student-centered learning, and the role shifts by teachers which make this new centering possible, are exemplified in the three "experiments" which follow.

In the first, a secondary social studies teacher describes the experiment herself.

A U.S. History Lesson: Sectionalism

The objective of the lesson was to introduce the issues of sectionalism in the 1820s and to allow the students to experience and participate in the legislative process.

The class was divided at random into three equal groups. The groups represented the three major sections of the country in the 1820s: the North, South, and West. Each student was given a handout which briefly described his or her section of the country. For example, a Northerner would be concerned with industry while a Southerner would be interested in agriculture. Each group was then instructed to create laws which they would want passed in Congress to benefit their section of the country.

The simulation game was played for two days with students writing, proposing, discussing, and voting on various proposed laws. Each time a group managed to have a law passed by the class which helped their section of the country the group was awarded points.

The following are examples of laws that were written and proposed by students during the simulation game:

1. From the North: Be it enacted that a tariff shall be charged and collected on all goods imported into these United States. The tariff shall be collected at the port of entry and shall amount to at least 50¢ on the dollar.
2. From the South: We the South propose that Congress be forbidden to discuss and consider the issue of slavery for the next 20 years.
3. From the West: We propose a motion that the Federal government use the income from the tariff for the construction of roads and canals in the west.
4. From the West: We want a law passed which would have the federal government remove the Indians to lands west of the Mississippi.
5. From the North: Be it enacted that slavery be excluded from newly acquired federal territories.

At the close of the game, it became evident that the North and West were working together and the South was not successful in passing any laws to benefit its section of the country. The

South, therefore, did not receive any points and the members of the group were angry and hostile. Some members even threatened secession from the union!

For homework, the students were asked to write on the following generalization:

Both nationalism and sectionalism developed after 1790, but by 1824 it was clear that sectionalism between the North, South, and West would dominate American life.

The purpose of this writing assignment was to find out what, if anything, the students had learned from the simulation game. Hopefully the students would agree with the generalization and discuss the various issues which were tearing the nation apart: slavery, the rate of the tariff, internal improvements at federal government expense, the chartering of a national bank, etc.

The objectives of the lesson were achieved. Students wrote essays which demonstrated that they had a clear understanding of what the word sectionalism meant and why it was a dominating force in the United States at this particular time. Instead of lecturing to the students about the issues of the time and how each part of the nation stood on these issues, they were given the opportunity to experience a given role and learn by way of role-playing. The essays written by the students proved that they indeed had learned.

Sectionalism between the North and West, on one hand and the South on the other dominated American life. The following essay will prove it.

Student Paper # 1

The South was very upset with what the North and West were doing. The North wanted a higher tariff and so did the West because of roadways and canals which were going to be built with the tariff money. But the South objected because they thought with higher tariffs England would put a tariff on their goods also, so they would have to pay for goods twice. They didn't care about canals because they had the Mississippi, Ohio, and many other rivers for transporting their products.

Another reason the South was going to secede from the nation was this issue of slavery. The North and West were against slavery. They had ralleys and protests to abolish it. But the South wanted slavery because they did many things for the rich plantation owners. They worked in the fields, they were servants and they took care of the land. So after some time they wrote a compromise for the "slave states" (the South) and the "free states" (West and the North), it stated that the property of Louisiana over 36° latitude were free and anything below that were slave states.

There were many reasons for the South to secede, but just for petty things. But those were the two main reasons.

The following essay has proved that sectionalism between the South and North and West would dominate American life.

Student Paper # 2

Both nationalism and sectionalism developed after 1790, but by 1824 it was clear that sectionalism between South and the West and North would dominate American life. I agree with this generalization to some extent. The sectionalism definitely dominated American life, but it wasn't always the South against the North and the West. It was sometimes the South and West against the North, and always the South against the North.

This is for many reasons. As we know, the three sections were very different; North having mostly industry and immigrants, West having small farms, Indians and some slaves, South having agriculture, large plantations and slaves. Having so many different needs, of course there was disagreement.

The difference in needs showed in many issues. For example, the Tariff. The North wanted high tariff to protect its industry. The West didn't need it, and the South didn't either because it exported. In this case the South and West were against the North.

Another example was internal improvement at Federal Expense. The North and the West wanted this because it helped their trade. South didn't want it because it didn't help them. In this case the South was against the North and West.

There was also disagreement on whether or not to have a National Bank. The North wanted it. They wanted state currency and to lend money. The West and South said "no"— there should be state banks as the money is easier to get. Again, this is the North vs. South and West.

Still another topic was slavery. Of course the South wanted it with their large plantations. But the North didn't want it because of their industry and because it was wrong, and West didn't have plantations.

Texas becoming a State was another subject of sectionalism. The South wanted it for more power in Congress. The West wanted it for farming. But the North didn't want another slave state.

I agree with the above generalization to some extent. There were definitely sectionalism between the North and the South, but not always between the North and West against the South. Sometimes it was the South and West vs. the North. This all dominated American life after all.

In the following essay it will be shown that sectionalism was more important than nationalism by 1824 and how sectionalism dominated the American way of life.

Student Paper # 3

Sectionalism occurs when inhabitants of certain regions of the country place their own specific need and well being above those of the nation. Nationalism on the other hand is a feeling of national unity in which people regardless of their own personal interest are willing to sacrifice these interests in order to preserve the union. . . . Both nationalism and sectionalism developed in 1790, however, by 1824 the United States had developed into three main groups: the South, North, and the West. On one side there was the South and on the other there was the North and the West. There are many reasons why these divisions occurred.

One reason has to do with the location in the United States itself. The southern part of the United States is ideal for growing crops and therefore is mainly agricultural. In the North, while there is some agriculture, it is mainly industrial. In the West it is predominantly small farms and the raising of live stock. Therefore, it is easy to see why the United States was beginning to divide. The second reason had to so with the issue of slavery. The South wanted to have slaves to do their work for them. The West which was partly composed of immigrants from Europe where slavery had already been abolished sided with the North. Other issues that were disputed between the North, South, and West were the issues of a tariff and of internal improvements. The South in both cases voted against these issues because they believed that it would only help the North and the West. Therefore this clearly shows that the country was moving from a feeling of nationalism to a feeling of sectionalism.

Obviously, the experiment included writing as the central use of language for learning. At the same time, talk of various kinds also played a key role. The activities of "proposing, discussing, and voting on various proposed laws" involved kinds of talk that were simultaneously essential for getting on with the simulation and for constructing knowledge of the issues. It seems likely, too, that the students' processes of learning the facts of regionalism in pre-Civil War America were underway before any writing occurred. In reality, the writing and talking fit into, and added, a particular instrumentality to an ongoing learning process which had already involved all uses of language including listening and reading.

Our next example comes from the work of a middle school science teacher. For some time in this eighth-grade class, she had experimented with students using poetic writing for learning. In a sense, this class had developed a "tradition" of story and poem writing within which Todd wrote the following play. The play is called *The Fantastic Voyage*, and Todd gives himself a starring role in it. Here is the play.

The Fantastic Voyage

Setting: An eighth-grade science classroom.
Cast of Characters:
MR. W. — school principal
MRS. G. — the eighth-grade science teacher
Eighth-graders: BILLY   STEVE
                DANNY   TODD
                JOEY   JIM
                SCOTT   MIKE

ACT I

The science classroom, where Steven is about to throw an eraser at Joey, is filled with eager, excited students.

MRS. G.: Steven! Put that eraser down right now or you'll be seeing a lot of Mr. Wydra today.
STEVE: Who? Me? I was just going to hand it to Scott to erase the board.
MRS. G.: That's what I thought. Do all of you have your permission slips? I wouldn't want any of you to miss this class trip.
CLASS: Yes, Mrs. Grabko.
BILLY: It's going to be fun visiting the human body to explore the digestive system!
MRS. G.: Yes, and I hope you all learn a great deal.
TODD: But, Mrs. Grabko, whose body are we going to visit?
MRS. G.: Well, yesterday Mr. Wydra volunteered to be the guinea pig, figuratively speaking, of course.

Mr. W. enters the classroom.

MRS. G.: Mr. Wydra!
MR. W.: (*Laughing*) Yes, I know. I agreed.

MIKE: So when are we going on the trip?

MRS. G.: Just as soon as you all take your shrinking pills.

MR. W.: But Mrs. Grabko, how would they do that? Will it hurt them?

MRS. G.: No, of course not. It will only shrink their body cells and tissues.

JIM: Will it hurt?

MRS. G.: Not a bit. You'll feel just like Alice did in Wonderland—a little strange, perhaps, but not hurt.

Mrs. G. hands out water and one pill to each student.

MRS. G.: Now everyone take a deep breath, put the pill in your mouth, and swallow it with the help of the water. Please be ready to step into the spaceship.

DANNY: How will we get into Mr. Wydra's mouth?

MR. W.: Oh, that's already taken care of. All I have to do is open my mouth and Mrs. Grabko will drive the spacecraft right into my body.

MRS. G.: All right now. Everyone come over here and let's take our pills.

The students gather around Mrs. Grabko and everyone does as instructed. Almost instantaneously they become so small they can hardly be seen. Everyone climbs into the spaceship which Mrs. Grabko had the foresight to set on the floor under her desk.

MR. W.: Mrs. G., is everyone all right?

MRS. G.: (*Just barely heard*) Yes, we're all okay.

MR. W.: Are you almost in the spacecraft?

MRS. G.: Almost. Hurry up students!

MR. W.: Now I will open my mouth. I will count to fifteen before I close it. One, two, three, four, five, six, seven, eight, nine, ten, eleven, twelve, thirteen, fourteen, fifteen. Ugh! They tasted like a mosquito!

ACT II

Inside the human body.

JOE: Mrs. G., where are we?

MRS. G.: Inside Mr. Wydra's mouth. This is the place where food enters the food tube.

TODD: What is that white bubbly stuff coming at us?

MRS. G.: It is only the juice of the saliva glands. It is called saliva and it begins the digestive process.

TODD: Those big white things must be the teeth.

MRS. G.: That's right. What are the top, the part under the gumline, and the lowest part called?

TODD: (*Pause*) The crown, neck, and, oh yes, the root.

MRS. G.: Right. How did you know?

TODD: I studied.

MRS. G.: Do you see that reddish thing moving over there?

CLASS: Yes.

MRS. G.: That is the tongue. Does anyone know how many kinds of tastebuds there are?

STEVE: Four.

MRS. G.: Correct. What are they?

JIM: Sweet, sour, salty, and bitter.

MRS. G.: What is the inner region of the tongue used for?

MIKE: The inner region is made up of muscles which push food from one side of your mouth to the other.

BILLY: (*Pointing*) What's that called?

MRS. G.: That's a salivary gland. It's secreting saliva. Does anyone know what a throat is?

TODD: It's the funnel that connects the mouth and gullet. Is that what we're sliding down now?

MRS. G.: Yes. The muscles near the base of the tongue and the muscular wall of the throat push food into the gullet. Does anyone know what that is called?

SCOTT: Swallowing.

MRS. G.: Right. Very good.

STEVE: Where are we going now?

MRS. G.: To the gullet which will take us to the stomach. Since we can't fly once we're inside the body, can anyone tell me how we will get there?

TODD: By way of a process called peristalsis. That means a wavelike motion moves the food, and us, along.

JIM: Mrs. G., look out! Here comes a slimy looking thing!

MRS. G.: Don't worry. That's just mucus which is secreted by mucus glands that line the inner surface.

MIKE: Where are we going now? It seems like we've moved on a J-like path?

MRS. G.: Yes, we have. We're in the stomach, which is shaped like a J. The stomach has three sets of muscles that push together and churn the food and push it into the small intestine.

DAN: I heard that there are some glands in here, too. Is that true?

MRS. G.: Yes, it is. Does anyone know what they are called?

JOEY: Gastric glands.

MRS. G.: Right. What do they do?

SCOTT: They secrete gastric juice and are located in the inner lining of the stomach.

MRS. G.: Yes, and what do they secrete?

STEVE: Enzymes called renin and pepsin, water, and hydrochloric acid.

MRS. G.: What does renin do?

TODD: It curdles the protein in milk called casein.

MRS. G.: Yes, and what does pepsin do?

TODD: It changes casein and other proteins into simpler substances.

MRS. G.: That's right, Todd. My goodness, you certainly *have* been studying! Who knows what water and hydrochloric acid do?

MIKE: They dissolve mineral salts.

MRS. G.: How did you know that?

JIM: Todd's been tutoring him.

Everyone laughs.

BILLY: If gastric juices secrete enzymes which break down the food, why don't they dissolve our ship?

MRS. G.: That's a very good question, Billy. We have a very special coating on this craft which repels the enzymes. Otherwise we'd be providing Mr. Wydra with lunch!

We are now about to enter the small intestine. Since it is 20 feet long, this will be a long part of our trip. It may also be turbulent, so fasten your seatbelts. Since the small intestine is like the gullet, they both have two sets of involuntary muscles and we will therefore be traveling by way of peristalsis.

JOEY: But Mrs. G., since all of the other organs have a special secretion, doesn't this organ have one?

MRS. G.: Yes, Joey, that's a very good question. The special secretion is pancreatic juice, secreted by the pancreas. It gets to the small intestine by way of a duct. The pancreas has several enzymes, but three are important. One of these changes starch into maltose. The other changes protein-like substances into amino acids, and the last one changes fat into fatty acids and glycerol.

BILLY: Can you tell us anything about the liver?

MRS. G.: Yes, Billy. It secretes the juice bile into the gall bladder which stores it.

DANNY: What about enzymes?

MRS. G.: It doesn't contain any, but it does change fat into tiny particles.

TODD: What is located in the inner lining of the small intestine?

MRS. G.: Intestinal glands.

JIM: What do they do?

MRS. G.: They secrete juice called intestinal juice.

MIKE: Are there any enzymes in it?

MRS. G.: Yes, there are four. One changes all protein-like substances into amino acids which complete the digestion of protein. The other three act upon carbohydrates and change them into glucose, thus completing the digestion of carbohydrates.

JOEY: You talked about all of these end products, but how do they enter the bloodstream?

MRS. G.: By way of absorption.

STEVE: But, I still don't understand how this happens.

MRS. G.: Well, since the lining of the small intestine has a very large surface in contact with the end products, it is particularly well suited to absorb them.

SCOTT: Todd told me something about the large intestine.

MRS. G.: What did he tell you?

SCOTT: He told me that undigested matter and water pass from the small intestine into the large intestine. Although it is smaller than the small intestine, it is greater in diameter. It is about five feet long and three inches in diameter.

MRS. G.   What does it resemble?

SCOTT: An inverted "U."

DANNY: But how does material move along it?

TODD: By way of peristalsis.

MRS. G.: Right, Todd.

JOEY: Mrs. G., isn't it about time to get out of here? This place is beginning to give me the creeps!

MRS. G.: Yes, Joey. It is time to leave. We are now in the rectum.

STEVE: Isn't that the place where solid wastes are stored until they are released from the body through the rectum?

MRS. G.: Yes it is, and here we go!

ACT III

MRS. G.: Well, here we are, safe and sound and our regular size again, thanks to the spinach pills. How did you like the trip?

CLASS: (*All speaking at once*) It was fun! Interesting! Exciting!

MRS. G.: Did you learn a lot?

CLASS: (*In a chorus*) Oh, yes!

MRS. G.: Good, because I want a nine-page composition on what we just learned by Friday. See you tomorrow!

CLASS: Bye, and thanks. Thank you, too, Mr. Wydra!

The bell rings and the students leave.

Curtain

The play's author has internalized the structure of class discussion. He knows how the teacher presents information, how she asks questions, and how she responds to students' questions and answers. In the form of a play, he recreates a process of thinking about science information which he has gotten from his class and others. He reconstructs in the dialogue the ways his teacher uses discussion to lead students to a full understanding of material, and he uses this structure himself both to understand the digestive system and to recreate his process of understanding in the play. He also borrows cleverly from the original Raquel Welch film of the same name, using its structure for his own purposes.

This student makes his understanding of the digestive system permanent by using it to invent this play, in which he assumes the role of a knowledgeable, hard-working, helpful student. In fact, before writing this play he had been a poor science student and in some trouble at school. We see him literally transforming his classroom role. And we see him coming to know this material more fully in order to create an enjoyable play. For him, the play's the thing, not the information, though he has had to get the information right to make the play work, just as he has had to get the dialogue structure right as well.

The final example comes from a secondary English teacher and includes two pieces of writing by the same student. The first is a paper on *Brave New World* and the second is a journal entry about the writing of the paper. Here are the two pieces.

To Lenina's Defense

Rather than judge the social standards in *Brave New World* to be moral or immoral, I would like to explore the morals of one character. It would be a futile attempt to refute the standards of the Alphas or Epsilons, as my morals, due to the environment and customs I was raised in, differ from those of other readers. Acknowledging this, I feel it better to adhere to a more persuasive topic, the defense of Lenina's morals.

Admittedly, when I first met Lenina, I mistook her for an ordinary pneumatic Alpha. She had all the characteristics of the average citizen — soma-addicted, spouted polished platitudes, was meat for any man, and seemed to have all the morals of a high-paid call girl. But, when considering that she, like every other Alpha or Epsilon, had acquired her morals through hypnotic repetitions, it occurred to me that her standards were no lower than her peers! So, why should it be unusual for her to throw herself at any man, especially John? Unfortunately, John had not been conditioned for this approach, rebuffed her advances, and beat her. My first inclination was to say, "Good for him. She deserves no less." My disgust soon turned to sympathy, for it was not any fault of Lenina, but simply the fault of her conditioning that caused her actions. When the most part of her associates were doing just what she had done, how could she not follow? Majority, after all, does rule.

Yet, Lenina was not like the majority, as she strived to make a type of commitment to her current lover. Four months of the same man was hardly acceptable in her time. Realizing this, she turned to Bernard, a character searching for something other than sex in a relationship. (General Hospital, here we come!) Then, John was the ultimate oddity, a person for whom Lenina actually felt . . . could it be (ugh!) love?

For this I believe Lenina to be the moral heroine. Although her promiscuous standards are not suitable for our society, they are in *Brave New World*'s utopia. As Herbert Spencer once said, "No one can be perfectly moral til all are moral." In *Brave New World*, all were moral.

Journal 6-1-82

I guess the secret to the *Brave New World* morals essay was lots of thinking and *procrastinating. Aha!* Every time I thought of writing it, I told myself, "No, think about it." Then I would decide until a little later to write. That went on for about 3 days. Then the weekend came. Home work on Saturday? Never! The idea of morals fascinated me, though, and I did quite a bit of thinking about my own. This lead me to putting myself in BNW's setting and I realized that my morals would have been obliterated in that atmosphere. I thought about Lenina and myself, drawing parallels where it was possible. Writing my columns of comparisons of my society to Lenina's also helped, but the key was looking up the quotations — I figured someone was bound to have already written what I felt — feelings I couldn't put to words. Sure enough, there was that person of great insight who wrote "in order for one to be perfectly moral, all must be moral." That set all the wheels in motion.

My first draft was down in 25 minutes. The next morning I reread it and decided it was far too stale, boring and cold — i.e., a typical 4 paragraph essay.

Since I had thought so much in Lenina's shoes, I thought — why not? I came to her defense and explained myself in the first paragraph. In all, it took 10 minutes to write, but hours to think about.

I suppose the People Express radio commercial prompted me to write in a straightforward personal way. The commercial goes something like this: "Do most airline commercials sound this way to you? We as an airline rule the skies, we rule the world, we rule you — I am the president of an important airlines every day and we fly every day which is why we want you to fly every day which is why we advertise every day etc. etc. . . . ."

They then go on to say that People Express is not couched in the suds and garb of other airlines.

I decided to simply state my feelings and observations in a journal like way. As you know, I'll do anything to get away from straight-laced, freshman year essays. (Conformity *is* one of my weaker points.)

(By the way, thanks for allowing us to do our own thing — it has helped me a lot. Sometimes it's too difficult to fill out a teacher's topic prescription, and sometimes it's just a lot more fun to work on your own ideas.)

This student has, as her journal entry suggests, learned a great deal through the process of writing the paper. She has certainly learned more about Lenina and about the society depicted in *Brave New World*. She has also learned more about writing: i.e., about how to do it so that it sounds the way she wants ("straightforward" and "personal"). Writing of various sorts has clearly played a key role in her learning, from writing "columns of comparisons" of her society with Lenina's to writing a first draft and a completely new second draft. Thinking and reading also played key roles, and it is the interaction among *thinking*, writing, and reading which created the learning and, for her, the satisfying piece of writing.

Interestingly, few students in this class had kept journals previously. The teacher required at least two entries per week and gave them a long list of possible topics for use at those times when they couldn't find one on their own. On Fridays, students brought their journals to class and shared some entries on a volunteer basis.

The teacher read and responded to each entry, establishing an open channel of communication by writing personal comments and by asking and answering questions. His intent was to get to know human beings. This journal procedure, he felt, was very effective. In his words:

I am guaranteed another role. I'm the encourager. It gives me a chance to listen, to be noncritical. Students get a chance to say what they want to say without being interrupted. I get a chance to learn, to know people, to see them as human beings . . . in intimate, open stances.

Further Discussion

Each of these students wrote a powerful piece by focusing on the comprehensive activity, the meaning of the whole. Each had a kind of super text, or whole meaning, "in mind" toward which she or he was working, and the super text remained the object of focal awareness throughout the composing. Moreover, each writer was committed to making this meaning. This unwavering focus on the whole meaning, the intended linguistic performance, was responsible, we are convinced, for the *quality* of the pieces. If the details, the elementary acts, of linguistic performance had become focal, if they had become the "to" rather than the "from," the quality of the whole would have suffered.

As Nancy Martin has suggested (1980, 1983), we owe it to our students to create the context for such committed performances. Frankly, when we create contexts in which our students begin to write *from their intentions,* we then owe them support for their unswerving focus on the whole meaning (or construct) they are making. We owe it to them not to deflect their attention from the whole meaning to the parts, at least not until they have the whole well in hand. We owe it to them not to require that they make the details of grammar or spelling or punctuation or diction a matter of focal awareness before they have, in effect, written a version (or versions) of the whole which pretty much satisfies them. Then, as readers of their writing, we owe it to them to construct a sense of what *they* are after, the whole *they* are working toward, and to direct our early responses toward helping them realize their intention. Otherwise, we will engage them in a destructive analysis of their performance, and what we will destroy *simultaneously* is the quality of the piece *and* the learning possibilities it offers. "What are they after, and how might I assist them in getting there?" are the questions we might best be asking, rather than more typical ones like, "How can I teach them this, or get them to do that, or make sure they get this other thing correct?"

Nancy Sommers (1982) illustrates this point, saying:

> The first finding from our research on styles of [teacher] commenting is that *teachers'* comments can take students' attention away from their own purposes in writing a particular text, and focus that attention on the teachers' purpose in commenting. The teacher appropriates the text by confusing the students' purpose in writing the text with her purpose in commenting.

And further:

> . . . after the comments of the teacher are imposed on the first or second draft, the students' attention dramatically shifts from "This is what I want to say" to "This is what *you* the teacher are asking me to do."

This shift happens most strikingly, she notes, when teachers identify errors in a first draft, regardless of whether they make meaning-oriented comments as well. Students generally choose to correct the noted errors rather than substantially reformulate the text, thus suggesting that they "see their writing as a series of parts . . . and not as a whole discourse." Therefore, we need to see their writing whole, in its full intention and direction, if we are to teach them to do the same. Assisting students in using language to learn with necessitates our staying focused clearly and steadily on students' intentions in using language and on the meanings they are using that language to construct and communicate. If we continue to ask whether they are getting the content or the skills right, our focal awareness will be on the elementary acts rather than on the comprehensive activity of their learnings: on where they are coming from, not where they are going to.

As Arthur Applebee (1981) noted in his nationwide survey of secondary-school writing practices, few teachers require students to do writing of paragraph length or longer. Only 31 percent of the 754 teachers who responded to the survey "reported *frequently* using such extensive writing tasks." And this "national figure" is qualified as "probably" an overestimate of "the extent to which such writing is used, since the teachers were nominated as 'good' teachers by their principals." The majority of teachers, as this survey and observations of classes in two midwest high schools indicate, normally use such writing activities as note-taking, copying, multiple-choice and fill-in-the-blank exercises, math calculations, and short answer responses requiring only a sentence or two.

> Analyzed as writing activities, such tasks are characterized by a separation of the problem of constructing coherent text in language appropriate to the subject area from the problem of remembering subject-area information and concepts. Essentially, the teacher takes over all of the difficulties inherent in using language appropriate to the subject area . . . and leaves the student only the task of mechanically "slotting-in" the missing information.

When we do this kind of thing regularly with writing, *we neglect students' intentions for writing almost entirely* and *eliminate almost completely* the learning potential of writing. Writing "can be a powerful process for discovering meaning rather than just transcribing an idea that is in some sense awaiting full development in the writer's mind" (Applebee, 1981). But this discovery of meaning occurs only, we contend, when the writing is sustained and continuous, when it reflects the writer's intentions, when it involves the writer in focusing steadily on the whole meaning to be constructed, and when the teacher supports these principles rather than subverting or denying them.

The pieces of student writing discussed earlier not only reveal learning occurring through the writing, as seen in the light of our model of learning, but they also reveal these other important principles of context at work. Each piece of writing is sustained, continuous prose; each aims at the creation of a whole meaning; and each grows directly out of the writer's intentions, including the pieces on "sectionalism." Although these students were writing in response to a fairly typical social studies assignment (there are some examples in Applebee, 1981, Chapter 4), as a result of the simulation they had a point of view and some relevant information. They constructed real arguments because they had real points to make.

Finally, each teacher supported his or her students in their particular processes of constructing and communicating knowledge. Each valued writing arising from personal intentions and expressing a personal response to experience. Each also valued writing in different modes and saw connections between different kinds of writing and learning. None of these pieces is typical of school writing. None fit the traditional school modes for informational writing, the kind of writing which dominates the school curriculum (Applebee, 1981; Parker, 1981, 1985; Tighe and Koziol, 1982). So, in fact, these students were supported in creating their own meanings and exploring modes of their choice. As a result, the writing produced learning and led to a transformation of experience.

Each of these teachers arranged the conditions for learning thoughtfully and skillfully. Each, also, took what these writers gave them and made intelligent and humane responses to the writers about their pieces. The pieces of writing and the comments on them were, truly, part of a larger ongoing dialogue between each teacher and these students. And, as we think you will see, each of the case studies which appears in the next chapter presents a similar though more detailed picture of these same principles of thinking, learning, planning, and responding at work.

4

Using Writing
in Five Courses

Writing in Entomology

Joseph Butchko, Professor of Entomology, is a self-made man. He earned his bachelor's degree over a 13-year period, while working full time. After obtaining his BA, he continued graduate studies in entomology while teaching at Mercer County Community College. Now a senior member of the faculty, he fascinates students and intrigues colleagues by the way he combines scholarship in his field and excellence in teaching with a variety of extracurricular interests which include activities as an outdoorsman and visiting teacher of nature studies in local area public schools, as well as summer grounds-keeper at the college. His quest for excellence is manifested in adventurous undertakings ranging from teaching entomology through poetry to enthusiastic participation in this project.

Butchko views learning as taking information that is presented in one situation and using it fully in another. He is particularly concerned about students' ability to take specific information and use it in other areas of school and/or life. "When you can handle that, I would think you're learning. We're talking about applying knowledge to a broader area than the one where the information is given."

To determine whether they are learning, he asks his students questions.

Hopefully, if I know that they've been in other courses, and some of the questions may relate to a vocabulary situation involving the information they received in another course, if they can apply what they learned in another course, such as vascular and woody plants to entomology, then I feel they're learning, and I'll ask them questions. For instance, we were discussing...

71

the functional unit of the nervous system, the neuron. . . . What
I attempted to do is to have them relate it to something they've
had, or something they should have . . . trying to show them
that it pays, that if you've spent a lot of time some place else
working on whatever you did, it is applicable in another area.
I continuously ask them questions; for instance, we discussed
the biconvex associations with the insect eye, and I'll ask: "If
you understand biconvex, what's biconcave?" and then I'll ask:
"What structure do you know in the human that's a biconcave
disk?" That's a red blood cell, and then we go into that. If they
can do this, I can pull a lot of it together.

I'll make a statement and ask: "What does it mean?" I'll have
them explain it. This sounds practical, but sometimes it's very
impractical. The kids are taking notes feverishly, and you stop
to ask them a question. They will have to take some time and
think about what they say. . . .

Sometimes he also makes deliberate wrong statements in his
lectures to test students' attention and to involve them in thinking
critically about content. In fact, he sees talk and writing as being
intertwined and interactive in the learning process. Thus, in discussions as well as with students' writing, he is alert for discrepan-
cies between his and their meanings, and he gauges his feedback
accordingly.

On the subject of personal writing, Butchko feels at a disad-
vantage.

I just don't do enough; I do write some letters; I correspond
with a few people and, I guess, there is note-taking . . . occasionally I will scribble down some poetry, but it's very personal,
only for me. I do lecture notes and little commentaries on my
lectures.

He has, for a long time, been writing to find what he thinks and
knows. As a student, he found that if he wrote when he studied, he
learned more of what had been presented to him. He made lists of
material he should know, When studying for an exam, he literally
sat and wrote out all his knowledge. He then checked what he had
written with his notes. This, he found, was the best way for him to
learn. First, he committed material to memory and then to prevent
not knowing it, he wrote it again and again until he felt he knew it.
He thinks that this writing contributed to the quality of his work.

I think writing is an excellent means of helping yourself gain a
great deal of knowledge. I don't know whether the act of
writing is so important, but reading what you wrote is important

because you can . . . say, "Oh my God, did I really want to say that?" By writing and reading the writing, you do a great deal of improving, and the end result is that you say what you should have said, instead of saying what you thought you said. . . . I use rereading to rethink.

Butchko's writing-to-learn strategies in his classes have developed gradually. He has always given essay examinations in entomology. Since being involved with the college's Writing Across the Disciplines Committee, though, he has increased the writing required in his classes.

I've always felt that writing is not only a good tool for students to learn, but it's an excellent tool for me. When I use it in testing, I can learn that, let's say, while you're writing a test question, it seems very obvious and straightforward to the writer; however, it apparently can appear very vague to the students. You find out that students are answering the questions differently from the way you expected them to.

He believes that one of his most important objectives, that of sending his students off to work or to other institutions with enough knowledge of entomology to be competitive or "on par" with their peers, is certainly strengthened by the writing tasks he requires. He also believes his students' analytic and critical thinking skills improve as a result of the writing they do in his course.

Predictably, Butchko favors a write-rewrite process. As a student, he rewrote his notes as soon as possible, and he thinks that is really what helped him through his studies. Writing is arduous and time-consuming, but he thinks rewriting is "very, very important." Moreover, he believes that any form of writing can be productive except, perhaps, assignments students do just to get them done. He is convinced that writing increases his students' problem-solving ability and learning. Writing forces them to organize their thoughts; and, as a result, students will cross out chunks of information and restate them. They think better, he believes, when they have to do that. His is a science course and "science involves organization. . . . The more organized you are in your thinking, the better off you'll be."

He tries to do things logically. He learns in "stepwise relationships," rather than "some of this and some of that." When he has to write, he does it as logically as possible: does an outline, learns it, then expands the outline. He was delighted by an off-beat example with a surprise ending in a recent student paper. He had asked his students to look philosophically at a specific problem in entomology and admitted sheepishly that the off-beat result was caused by a poorly written question. He had expected the answer to be purely entomological. This particular student answered the question of metamorphosis philosophically, which led Butchko to believe that the student was able to take information learned someplace else, put it together with entomological information, and answer the question quite reasonably.

In giving students written responses to their papers, Butchko comments on vague statements as well as incorrect grammar. If the problem of vagueness is serious, he holds a conference with the student. There, he typically asks:

> How would you grade this question (based on the question versus the answer)? They may know what they're saying, but they must be able to convey it to me because ultimately, I may have to grade them on what I think they're saying. However, I do not assign a value to every comment I make on a question. Occasionally, I'll have them write something in class; I'll just stop and have them write something on a piece of paper, and everyone is required to make a statement. Even if they don't understand, they have to write something, and I look at it, and I talk to them about the answer. I don't collect it, I just want them to do some writing.

Thus, he appreciates the potential of spontaneous, unevaluated writing and realizes that it encourages student risk-taking and, thus, creative or connective thinking.

In using writing to complement learning through other classroom and laboratory activities, he asks students to follow a three-step procedure. First, students go out into the field in teams to record environmental data, such as temperature and humidity readings, and to note their insect findings. These data are recorded briefly on index cards. Then, students are asked to convert these brief notes into expanded and more detailed narratives. Upon their return to the next laboratory session, they transfer this expanded information onto formal data sheets, with space provided for both quantitative and qualitative data.

> Students have a tendency to look at insect collecting as a lark. However, doing the writing of lab reports in stages now makes it more serious. Sometimes it becomes a bit of a problem: we're out there with collecting jars plus writing equipment, and we do some data collection to make the lab reports meaningful. But I do think it does fortify what's going on in lab. It does make it much more meaningful, now that they gather up all this information and put it in writing in stages.

In his lectures Butchko urges students to take notes and then to condense their notes by selecting the essence, thus encouraging learning as a process of contraction and abstraction. Thus, he sees writing as useful for making connections. As we shall see in the cases of Margaret and Bill, he supports his students in using writing to apply learning gained in one area to another and to move from factual to philosophical considerations. He recognizes the importance of sequencing intellectual and writing tasks, obliterating arbitrary subject matter boundaries and bridging the gap between disciplines to eliminate pigeonholing of knowledge.

Margaret's Writing

Margaret was in the minority at the college. To this day, few women take "serious" science courses here or in other community colleges. Judging from her concentration, interest, and precision, Margaret functioned well in the entomology class. Though uncertain about her specific career goal, she knew that she wanted to work in some aspect of the biological sciences.

Her recent writing-to-learn activities had included answering end-of-chapter or end-of-text questions in chemistry and biology textbooks. In entomology, Margaret felt writing helped her master and remember many facts, including a lot of terminology.

Field notes help in several ways. We bring the specimens into the lab and study the mouth, digestive tract, internal parts—we really couldn't learn from the book. Writing the objectives for field work, I learn the terminology and what to expect in the dissection; to know which way we are going. It helps to listen (in class/lab) and write about it and to see it, you have parallels.

She explained that moving in steps from writing brief field notes, to writing expanded narratives, and to writing organized lab reports helped her to think more fully about the data. Sometimes, with the brief notes, Margaret would ask, "What's this?" then really try to understand, think about it, and put things in perspective. Then, as the writing progressed from "ladybug on blade of grass," to a more complete description, to the accepted lab format, complete with scientific terminology, she could really understand the initial material.

In a general biology course, taken before entomology, writing was used more than any other strategy. "He [the instructor] would give us written objectives, and in recitation we could discuss these objectives and our answers to them." Margaret not only remembers more when she writes things down but also understands them better, too. "But it's messy, at first." This messy process is a necessary stage of confusion in the process of understanding and learning.

When Margaret attends a lecture, she takes copious notes. Then, she attempts to "translate" these rough notes. She begins by reading them to remember what the class was discussing. Next, she unites the parts of the lecture that belong together.

> One part of a unit here and another there just won't do for learning purposes. . . . If I didn't rewrite the notes, I wouldn't find the connections. I'd hate to sit there during the test and say, "Now, where was the other part of this?"

She finds reconstructing her notes, aided by the question-answer format of unit objectives, helpful in learning to think and write in the special language of the discipline she is studying. Generally, her learning process entails finding everything and just writing it down. Subsequently, she is able to put it together. Margaret tries to do all of this work at one sitting. Once she enters her learning process, she feels, it is better for her to concentrate on just the one task. She also likes to ask the same questions in different ways. As a result, she asks questions while studying. Some of them are directed at her teachers, and others she answers by herself.

Finally, after having taken an unabridged set of notes and revising them, Margaret prepares a final condensed and abstracted version, reaching for the essence of the material. This final version serves to organize the new information in a form that she can fit into her existing knowledge. She feels that the carry-over into daily life is manifested primarily in heightened powers of observation and an ability to analyze, to dissect problems into their component parts.

Margaret's laboratory-related writing in entomology illustrates her learning process. Her 9/8/81 entry in her field notebook indicates that Pat recorded the air temperature at $72\,^{\circ}$F and relative humidity at 90 percent while Joe determined wind velocity at 0 miles per hour and soil temperature eight inches below the surface at $70\,^{\circ}$F. Elmer measured the soil pH at 6 beneath an overcast sky. The group defined the "ecosystem" as "open field followed by woods." Margaret's team found quite a harvest: a "bee dying on the road," "grasshoppers in the weeds of the field near the woods," "termite on log," a "big beetle with big hairy mandible in tree stump under bark" (perhaps a "vest beetle"), a "black H20 beetle, or cockroach, in rotting wood," an "insect off of goldenrod that looks like a lightening bug on top, with a bee's abdomen," and a "black wasp that was on goldenrod, caught walking on ground."

These bits of descriptive information were expanded into a narrative in which the "insect . . . that looks like a lightning bug on top, with a bee's abdomen" becomes "A group of flying insects that had markings similar to those of a lightning bug, with a yellow and black stripe on the abdomen was gathered on a patch of goldenrod"; the "black wasp that was on goldenrod . . ." becomes "the black wasp who fluttered its wing repeatedly was captured while walking on the ground after flying from goldenrod."

This information, in its edited form, is then neatly transferred onto a formal lab report sheet:

NAME: Margaret E. Secks		LOCATION: Mercer Co. College
DATE: 9-15-81	AIR TEMP: 72°F	TIME: 2-5 pm
RH: 90%	SOIL (pH): 6	The ecosystem was an open
SOIL TEMP: 70°F	WIND: 0 mph	field surrounded by wood

FIELD NOTES

p. 7
The large bee was found dying on the dirt road.

The grasshopper was in the weeds of a field near the forest's edge.

The vest beetle, a large black insect with sizeable mandibles was under the bark of a tree stump.

The termite and the small black beetle (possible a cockroach) were found in the rotting wood of a log.

p. 8
A group of flying insects that had similar marking of a lightning bug with a yellow and black abdomen was gathered.

Through this process, in which writing and rewriting is a central activity, Margaret constructs (and reconstructs) her knowledge of entomology. She moves from experience recorded in her own language toward a formulation of that experience presented in the specialized vocabulary and format of the science of entomology. Importantly, she gains her knowledge by doing something with it, making new versions of it, through writing. We call this process *expansion*: Margaret has expanded her formulations of field trip experience from brief, sketchy, field notes to a polished, complete lab report through these three stages of writing and rewriting.

Margaret also learns through a process, centrally involving writing, which we call *contraction*. This process is illustrated by three drafts of her class notes on the insect thorax.

[First Draft]

1. The thorax is the central portion of the insect body consisting of 3 segments: the (anterior) prothorax, the mesethorax, and posterior-metathorax. The apterygotes 3 thoracis segments are structurally similar in that the tergem and sternum are plate like throughout and the pleural sclerites are small or degenerate. In the pterygotes, the thoracic segments are dissimilar. The peothorax is essentially the basic condition, general separate and less developed from the other segments although it can be large and ornate and metotorax are very complex having combining both the running & flying abilities. The sub-coxa (or pleuron) is extended

2. The functions of the thorax are mainly for movement by which is accompanied by legs and wings.

3. The Sclerotized plates and sutures of the thorax are
Dorsal Surface
The thoracic tergum or notum of the pterygotes is more complex than that of the apterygotes. In the pterygotes the lere notum was divided into smaller plate (sclerites by various suture associated with the evolution of wings and flight. Generally, the pteroth (wing-gearing segments) is composed of 2 parts.

(pteratherusic)
Alinotum — The anterior portion of the tergum segment directly associated with wing attachment. The alinotum has an anterior apodeme, an or phragmd. The alinotum is the sclerite connecting directly with the wing.
Postnotum—The posterior portion of a pterothorax. It is connected laterally with the epineron, (ventral to the postnotum), forming a bridge just posterior to the wings. It bears a posterior phragma which is larger than the anterior apotems of the alinotum. The post phragmal portion of the postratum is usually part of the next posteria segment which has become a functional part of the seg anterior segment.
Thorax —Composed of 3 segments

anterior	pro	
	mesor	thorax
posterior	meta	

functionally the thorax is the locomotive lgr tagma because it bears the legs and wings ~~of~~if they have them.
Wings—associated with mesal and meta, if present, collectively called pterothsas.
In most winged insects the prothorax is generaly separate and less developed from other segments with wings. Can be large and ornate but not complex.

[Second Draft]

insects (Hymenuptera) 1st 2 abdominal segments becomes closely associated with thorax.

Each segment divided into 4 parts
  Corsally:
    turgum
    notum
  Ventrally:
    sternum
  Lateral:
    Pleura

[Third Draft]

1. The 3 parts of the thorax are the:
   prothorax
   mesa-thorax
   meto thorax
2. The second & third segments of the thorax are associated with the wings (meso & meto)
3. The notrum or thurgum
4. pterothorax—meso & meto thorax wings bearing portion of the thorax

Each time she returns to the material, she selects, focuses, and reorganizes what she had previously written. Her original notes (first draft) are somewhat jumbled, lacking any clear organization. The second draft is much briefer, a skeletal outline really, and it seems to reflect her search to identify the key elements and to conceptualize their relationships simply, economically, and accurately. The third draft, though also much briefer than the first, is expanded slightly beyond the second by the use of some sentence-type formulations. It is also personalized, reflecting what *she* knows rather than what is out there to be known. This sequence of drafts, we think, represents learning by contraction and, simultaneously, making personal knowledge.

Throughout her writing and in her interviews as well, Margaret displays a clear, personal sense of direction in her choice of writing-to-learn activities. For her, writing encourages observation: "You have to know what you're looking for or at to write about it." It also focuses attention, forces thinking, and fosters analysis. She uses it for integration and organization of subject matter and recognizes its value in producing flashes of insight (especially in the revision phase). And finally, she sees writing as interacting usefully with listening and talking.

Bill's Writing

Bill, a quiet young man, willingly shared not only his written work in entomology, but also his writings in sociology and economics. He even made special trips to deliver missing or misplaced material and to share his thoughts on writing to learn. Over the years, in various subjects, Bill has developed a number of writing-to-learn strategies. Like Margaret, he takes notes copiously and indiscriminately, and then he rewrites them to clarify his understanding and to make connections.

> In mathematics, I always write problems out over and over. The best way for me to study is just to rewrite the material. When I take the notes, I don't concentrate too much on them; when I retake them I can sort of relate one type of material to another and then I refine it a little bit. Yes, it does help me learn when I rewrite my notes of entomology.
>
> I usually also write marginal notes when I don't understand something. You probably noticed more marginal comments in my rough notes. That's when I'm not sure about something and don't want to interrupt him [the instructor] and ask him exactly what he means. I write myself a little note so I can check on it later on. Or sometimes, when he explains it in class, I want to make sure that I understand it the same way I understood it when he gave the lecture, so I write myself a note to keep me on the right track when I go to read my notes later. I do this for most of my classes: I write and then keep on grinding away at it until I understand it.

Commenting on other ways of writing to learn, Bill speaks about the advantages of an outline.

> I don't go into too much depth; I just put in the stuff that I think I may have difficulty with (I go over that a little more carefully) plus the other material into my own words, so that I can understand it better.

He also likes to make lists. For example, when his entomology instructor explained certain things, he numbered the remarks and put them in columns. "For me, it's easier to learn in vertical rows. I don't know why. . . ."

Bill writes in organic chemistry, too, but not in the same ways. In this case, he writes to test himself.

> I just keep writing it to see if I got it correct. . . . I also write summaries for myself in organic chemistry. Like I said, we have a lot of reactions and I just write down how and why

things are happening. Then I won't forget it so quickly. When I go to studying it, the summaries make it a little simpler.

No one really forced him into writing. He has been doing it ever since he knew that it helps him learn. If he writes before each test, it helps him: "When the final comes, I don't feel like I'm in the dark. I put the little notes in the margin, so that I can get back on the original track if I seem to be a bit confused."

About economics, he says:

I take down notes that will help me, what I feel is relevant. You notice a lot of times, I seem to repeat stuff over and over. I do that because there is a slight difference I want to distinguish later.

In sociology, it's quite different. You can go a whole day and take down only one or two words. What the instructor talks about is common sense, so I just put down specialized terms and lists of things that would not be common knowledge. I answer his questions on the course objectives for each unit.

In contrast to sociology, Bill's archaeology class required large amounts of writing, including work on assigned topics such as tribes of Indians. Students had to research these topics and write four- to five-page reports. He felt this writing helped him master the material he had researched, but it did not necessarily help him to relate this material to anything covered in class.

Writing takes a lot of time, and you run the thoughts in your mind a lot. Automotically, you keep thinking about the material and it gets embedded in your brain somehow, so you won't forget it so easily.

Bill often uses writing as a steppingstone to further thinking, "to aid in going more in detail, deeper into studying. Definitely, that's why I write. With my entomology, I do that in steps as I go along." In this process, Bill asks questions and writes reminders. In fact, he has a page in some of his notebooks just for reminders. Sometimes he asks the teacher a question taken from a reminder. For example, his sociology notes are heavily annotated and filled with marginal comments referring both to other self-writings or to external textual sources related to the subject matter under discussion. All of his notes show this process to make connections. In addition to annotating his notes and making marginal comments, Bill complements, expands, and elaborates on his class and laboratory notes with examples or restatements. Speaking of the concept of a "total institution" while reworking the notes, Bill added "Army." In expanding the notion of "quantification" as one of the steps of the scientific method, Bill adds the clarification: "creating standard units for measurement." "Measurement," he then adds, "is using these standards to compare."

Bill also stars essential ideas and concepts, both as a selection mechanism and a reminder for further study, as in defining the Sapir-Whorf hypothesis in sociolinguistics. He shows relationships with arrows. In discussing "criteria for determining social class," Bill writes, "*also see notes of October 15 and October 22." Having defined "cultural integration" as the "degree to which various elements of a culture are interrelated and form a distinctive pattern," Bill notes, "*also see notes on values." Elaborating on one aspect of culture, "custom," he adds to the original version: "any other capabilities (in addition to knowledge, belief, art, mores, law and habits) required by man as a member."

To this diagram of a bilateral family unit,

$$
\begin{array}{ccc}
\overline{\hspace{6cm}} & & \\
= 0 & & \underline{\hspace{1cm}} = \\
\overline{\hspace{2cm}} & & \overline{\hspace{2cm}} \\
= 0 \quad \underline{\hspace{1cm}} = & & = 0 \quad \underline{\hspace{1cm}} = \\
\overline{\hspace{2cm}} & \overline{\hspace{2cm}} & \\
= 0 \quad = \quad = 0 & & = \\
\underline{\hspace{1cm}} & \underline{\hspace{1cm}} &
\end{array}
$$

Bill adds "* if not bilateral, only connected through one side to complete the picture with implied comparison/contrast." In differentiating between French population units of 2,000 and United States units of 2,500, he completes his understanding by adding the marginal note "to be classified as urban."

In economics, while discussing the gross national product, he comments (in reworking the notes) that "if per-capita income increases, we are all better off because productivity has increased," thus drawing implications from what started out as a simple definition. To the explanation of "short-run" and long-run" market, he writes in the margin "economists differ" to indicate that the concepts are certainly not universally accepted. He also uses verbal notations to clarify graphs of "full employment economy."

In entomology, Elmer, Saileh, and Kristina were Bill's lab partners. Like Bill, each expanded their field entries as they transferred the information onto official forms. All team members shared responsibility for gathering initial information. The grasshopper that Bill found on 9/8/81, on an 84 °F day, with 66 percent relative humidity came from "a grassy area near the theater of MCCC" and was "four inches in length." Saileh and Kristina measured the soil temperature at 73 °F, while Elmer provided the wind measurement as 6–8 mph from the south-southeast. The report noted that the soil pH was not measured, and that the field work lasted from 2:15 to 4:15 p.m.

In the rough draft of his detailed description of the grasshopper, Bill stated: "The thoracic and the first two abdominal spiricles open during expansion and close during contraction which means inhalation occurs anteriorly and exhalation occurs posteriorly." Alongside, in the margin, in different colored ink, he wrote, "Ask Elmer!" Having described the rows of spiricles on the mese- and meta-thorax, Bill mentions the presence of eight spiricles on the abdomen. Next to the latter tentative comment, Bill remarks, "Count them."

In his lecture notes, Bill describes "cells that are circular and elliptical in cross-section." However, he must have had his doubts because he writes in the margin, "Messed up?" A bit farther along, in continuing his treatment of the cellular system, Bill notes again in the margin, "More?" "See Elmer on mitotic division" is the next admonition, along with "know common scientific names." In the margin of a description of "thinning, branching processes called dendrites" is the notation "tree-like structures," the very example used by Butchko, whose definition of learning is the application of knowledge gained in one field to another. In this case, the application uses the concept of the tree-like structures common in the study of vascular and woody plants to another aspect of entomology.

Bill's field notes represented the open exploratory phase of learning, with writing acting as means or instrument. Writing helped Bill observe more clearly, extend his awareness of natural phenomena via group atmospheric readings, and produce detailed descriptions of various insects. It also helped him to raise and answer questions about lecture and lab material, seek further information or clarification, make connections, and remember both information and operations. Like Margaret, Bill is aware to some extent of the various instrumental roles that writing is playing in his learning. Not only is writing helping them construct knowledge, but it is also helping them construct a theory of learning, one which they both are becoming more able to articulate.

Margaret's and Bill's classmates in entomology also agreed on the value of writing to assist learning. These students confirmed that, while going over material orally or visually may be momentarily effective, writing it out offers greater assurance of permanent learning. Their preferred writing activities included scribbling key words for later elaboration, outlining, defining terms, formulating questions for self or teacher, and restructuring class notes in various ways.

Most of them also prefer essay exams. They say, "You can't just get by; it shows how much you know without guessing," and "In an essay exam, I can develop something; in a multiple choice, if I lose that one word, everything falls apart."

Writing, these students feel, promotes direct, multisensory contact with material: seeing it, writing it, reading what they have written, and rewriting it. The kinds of writing used in entomology, they think, promote "chunking" of material into manageable portions. Marginal notes are praised for giving essential hints and helping to complete a picture, and flashcards and multiple drafts are also popular. In the words of one class member, "Writing is the only way I know [the material] and know that I know it."

Writing in Clinical Nursing

As a nursing educator with many years of clinical and teaching experience, Claire Raimondo is equally committed to instructing the science and art of nursing and to nurturing her students as fledgling practitioners and as individuals with unique strengths, weaknesses, and problems. As part of this commitment, she has had a long-standing interest in improving her students' communication and critical thinking skills through writing.

Her first priority is teaching her students in a way that encourages thinking. She feels they cannot function without being logical and organized in their thinking, especially because they will often be called upon to deal with crisis situations. Raimondo wants also to instill confidence. She wants them to know that they can train themselves to think and learn and handle situations. "Then," she says, "I can get in and whet their appetite for more."

Raimondo writes frequently, both in her personal and professional life.

In my work situation, I'm writing all the time. I don't write "finished," edited papers. When I think of something I may want to put into a clinical objective, I just jot it down at what I call "inspirational times." I may be driving to the clinical area, and I get into the office. Early mornings are my best times and while I'm waiting for the students, I'll say, "Oh, let me write that down." Later I go back and start to elaborate on it, follow up on it, to see if it was a reasonable idea. "Would it turn students on to learning?" So I'm very much of a note-taker. At home, I have notes all over the place; little reminders to organize my day. It's a joke in the family. I have to confide that I may wake up out of a sound sleep at 3:00 a.m. when I have a project going on or coming along; I will think of a phrase or an idea and jot it down on a pad by my bedside.

She feels that writing provides good "mental exercise" and keeps her on top of things. "I use it all the time on the hospital floors. I walk around with a note pad in the pocket of my lab coat. In nursing, it's a consistent thing: we write charts every day. . . ."

To Raimondo, learning occurs through active participation. "Learning is an active process; it isn't just sitting there complacently. I allow students time to observe and listen, and I take them there. I try not to pressure them during pre- and post-clinical conferences, and it pays off. We wrap up the day with student feedback and their writing about it. Then they share their written notes. Time and again I hear, 'I learned so much from my classmates' experiences.'"

She began using writing extensively with her students when she first started teaching in the labs. She then initiated the idea of student pre- and post-clinical conferences. Although she found to her dismay that few students really knew how to write very well, she was impressed by their eagerness to learn. To Raimondo, writing strengthens many learning objectives, not the least of which is elimination of the "fear of that blank piece of paper" and combatting learning-by-rote memorization.

> Factual information is certainly important; it's like the alphabet, but the synthesis and thinking process, to me, are much more important. You have to be able to say, "Now what's going on? How am I going to be able to handle it? What's happening inside of me? Am I arriving at the right conclusion?" The secret of nursing is to have confidence in your ability to think. Thinking is an involved process; nursing students must go through all the steps until the pieces of the puzzle fit and they can say, "I understand." Nursing judgment is what we're talking about.

Raimondo observes students' clinical activities, then requires them to summarize what they learned from that experience. If students are not required to do some form of written "highlighting," their learning is less thorough. Typically, she asks for brief written answers to questions such as: "What do you think of this experience? If you were to do it again, what would you change?" These questions encourage students both to speculate and to draw conclusions from their experience.

> I find that by the students' sitting down to write, even if it's only a line or two, it reinforces learning because they have to synthesize. They have to look back and say, "Now, what did happen today? What did I learn, and what did I get out of this?" If it's in writing, I really find it more practical than just talking about it.

She realizes she cannot give everyone identical writing experiences even though she has a "master plan" and tries to select three or four students to do a learning activity and another two or three to do a clinical activity on any given day. "When they come back to the group, they share learning experiences that have basic principles, and this is what we discuss. We find this effective. There is no way they could all participate in the same learning experiences. This way, you get evaluation and inferences from shared writings." Raimondo's master plan extends to preparing the ground on which her students will walk (and work).

Our academic calendar starts in September, but I visit agencies the last week of August or so and meet with people I plan to work with. We sit down and talk about it. "This is what we did last year. Was it effective? What can we do to improve it?" So there were reams of work sheets I used last summer.

Raimondo spends one to two hours with each person. Then she determines what would be the best type of learning in all the possible areas in which her students will be working. She goes back to what they had the previous year: where they were in their learning and what she could make more up-to-date, add, or subtract. Decisions include,

what areas I am going to use clinically; what key person I am going to work with so we can do preplanning together. That's the most critical: planning, then implementing the tentative plan. As soon as I get one group through, I call and visit again to find out how things were viewed as working out. I need to get personal feedback.

Her bridge from master plan to goals and objectives involves assignment design, both oral and written. She is aware of what students have had and builds on it: on the film they have seen and on the tapes she has developed for their use. She picks them up from that point and reinforces the basic learning they have had.

When they say, "Mrs. Raimondo, we see the book come alive in the clinical setting," I have found what I aim for. My main purpose is what I want a nursing student to understand about this particular patient who has this particular problem of suspicion, withdrawal or whatever the semester's laboratory objective may be. I focus on that particular area; I try to narrow it down. Since I don't know my students before I get them in the clinical area, I never assign tasks too far in advance. I know what areas I'm going to use. After I meet them for a day or two, and I get the feeling that, "Aha, this students needs a challenge," then I go through the roster and make assignments. I have to be selective and do a lot of shifting around as I get to know the person. At preconference, I pick up that some are ready for a particular assignment and others are not. I try to support the weaker student. Individualization is what I aim for; for those that I didn't get to, I put a little reminder, an IOU for the next module. "I owe this student this or that experience to complement what the others have had." I try to give them all an opportunity. I am very structured in that I plan every action, but then I am flexible in the implementation.

The preclinical conference, Raimondo feels, is her responsibility. The day before she selects clients for the students, and posts the assignments in their mailboxes so that they can do a little research on their case.

The next morning, when everyone is uptight, I introduce them to their clients. Then, in preconference, I say, "Pull out your papers, and let's see, how many of us have the diagnosis of a paranoid schizophrenic?" (Of course, I have their papers right in front of me.) "Mary, why don't you start and, Emily, you add something." There's sharing of what they learned the night before in their textbooks. After 30 to 45 minutes, we have covered everyone's diagnosis. But if we didn't, I'll say, "Why don't you save your papers and bring them back to post-conference. Maybe we'll get to them then. I know you have spent a great deal of time on this material. In the laboratory, let's focus on these skills (or those principles). If you bring your papers back again, some of us may find we have had the same types of assignments. With a little experience on the second day, we'll see some changes." That makes them feel they're going to add to their knowledge.

There are other ground rules as well. Once she makes it clear that she doesn't want to hear identical comments the second time, students go into greater depth. "We deal with drugs, medications, and everything just flows. I'll say, 'Well, that side-effect was interesting; what did you find?'"

The clinical papers assigned are outgrowths of these clinical assignments. Every student gets a form with the patient's initials, diagnosis, and medication. They pick these up and do some research the night before. They have to complete a column on "nursing responsibility" and do a "drug card" on every drug assigned. They also do evaluations on patients. These are done on clinical time and are not taken home. When they take a break, they write notes on their client interviews.

After they return from lunch, Raimondo allows them a half hour to write and do charts or worksheets. These help her diagnose where each of them is in their ability to observe, record, and report on the patient's behavior and on changes they have observed. "In psychiatry, that's the only way to go." Then she can see them individually and share suggestions and comments.

In the post-conference interview, Raimondo gives students 15 to 20 minutes to work on their assessment sheets.

I flip a name card and say, "Why don't you paint a visual picture of your patient for us from your notes?" The ground rule is that they may read only what they wrote. They are usually delighted to find that they could write well enough to paint a vivid picture of appearance and behavior. Post-conference deals with word pictures. If I collected their notes, they would only be sharing with me. It is a much more effective learning tool to have the students sharing among themselves.

Another written activity she uses is a "problem-severity scale for psychiatric nursing." It outlines such problem areas as emotional or marital problems. The students circle a number from 1 to 6, and at the post-conference, paint another picture based on the question: If you were the nurse, what would be the priority needs of your client and what would be your nursing interventions?

The problem-solving paper was created when Raimondo wanted something that would tell her about the nursing judgment of her students. She needed to find out what kind of a paper could help a student grow in an unfamiliar area. The original purpose was to induce the student to say: "This happened. . . . How did I handle it? If it happened again, what would I do?" Raimondo took this assignment design directly to the patient situation. Initially, the student would discuss how well he or she handled the first day at the mental facility. Having found long papers a source of irritation to the students and herself, Raimondo refined this to a two-page assignment, the significance of which lies in the student's perception of what was learned from a particular experience. She knows that in a short assignment students must be selective and must interpret their experience.

Raimondo feels that such writing increases problem-solving ability, particularly in clinical situations in which there are collaboration and multiple feedback. The whole class benefits from such shared experience. Since she also attributes great importance to writing for personal problem-solving, she gives students a choice between a problem-solving paper reflecting a nurse/patient or a nurse/ self relationship. "I get quite a few of the second variety. They will say, 'I didn't know I could change my feelings about . . .'" This type of writing has a great impact.

She tries to match writing tasks with educational goals. She is especially concerned about the stressfulness of psychiatric interviewing and counseling. Consequently, when she teaches them, she designs tasks that train students in writing up the interview in retrospect. This involves recalling: "What was it that I did? And why did I do it?" On her interview forms, there is a column for comments. That is where a student may realize she goofed if all the patient gave was a "yes" or "no" response. Throughout, students are applying theory and thus understanding the theory better through reflecting on its applications in the written interview reports.

> I don't have to pull out a book and say, "Did you notice this?" Listening to that patient, sitting with him/her, feeling the psychic hurt of the patient: all are important. The case of the "mythical patient" may be debunked by, "A marvelous process paper! Who is your patient?" Another plagiarized paper bites the dust!

Raimondo considers this process report her most effective writing assignment, particularly the column on rationale and commentary.

> If they say, "This really worked for me," I've gotten them to where I want them. Interest is then transferred to nursing notes and charts. Now they're not blocking at the sight of a blank piece of paper. On their little note pads in their pockets, they have their short morning notes. The first time around when they come to me, I say, "This is good; let's take five minutes to share it even before we go into the conference room; now you read . . ." Then they start, together, changing and editing. By the time they get to the charts to put the information down, they have polished it. Essentially, they do it in drafts, learn by doing; they get confidence and receive praise from the staff of the institution.

Thus, students participate in a variety of practical and intellectual tasks by means of diverse types of discussion and writing. The writing, they feel, helps them in conducting focused observations of patients, in assessing situations, and in planning individualized nursing intervention. It increases their therapeutic effectiveness by leading to more active listening, helping them to understand how patients perceive situations, to reflect upon these situations, and to formulate open-ended questions designed to gather more information. They work through daily dilemmas, trying out their nursing wings.

As these interviews illustrate, a teacher who values writing to learn, in the context of valuing good teaching, will encourage her students to use writing variously in many learning contexts. And Raimondo's endorsement of writing as a means of learning is not just a lightly held pedagogical belief, for she herself uses writing to fit new knowledge into an existing framework, to give and receive feedback, and to paint precise word pictures. In her personal and professional life, she finds that writing often triggers and results in flashes of insight. She believes in the use of writing for self-examination, for application of theoretical knowledge, and for learning about the self and the world.

Kathleen's Writing

Kathy, an enthusiastic young woman in her early twenties, worked as a licensed practical nurse before enrolling in the nursing program. Now she is eager to learn the more academic aspects of nursing.

Kathy has long been aware of the value of writing, as evidenced by her personal journal writing before starting college.

When I write, I can see changes, and it means a lot more to me when I can reflect on things I've done, places I've been. The best way I can do that is through writing. Of course, you can pick up a book and associate with what's written in it, but it's not like seeing it in your own handwriting: "I had such a good time" or "I was disappointed here." Not only that, but I can tell from my handwriting when I've had good days or bad days. On good days I tend to write neater and smaller. If I'm upset or in a hurry, it gets larger and harder to understand.

Now, she keeps a journal, although not regularly. She writes in it only at turning points in her life. When she looks back on these occasions or events, she feels she has learned a great deal. "It's not information I need to get a job, but information about me, and I see where I have changed. I can see what was important then, and I think, 'Was that a priority? Now it means nothing.' I see where I have grown through that."

In her interviews, Kathy said that she had done her most significant writing to learn in her math classes, to get things clear in her mind. More than in any other subject area, she needed to have things documented and to have a plan of action. ". . . step 1, step 2, then I could see where I had gone wrong, or where I needed work. Chemistry was another example where I could understand things better if I wrote them down. Writing makes me more proficient and a lot more alert to little things."

She composes questions for later use in every subject, even mathematics: "'Ask X why this goes before that?' I'll write it out and feel more comfortable that way." She writes some of these questions in preparation for discussion. She feels her thoughts are not well organized when she has a lot of material to cover since she tends to skip from personal experience to fact to other people's

experience. Consequently, she finds preparatory written notes beneficial. The material she wants to get across to others becomes better
organized and formulated that way. She also writes summaries to
remember discussions.

> I did that today when we were talking about different drugs.
> I remember I wrote down some information on "digitalizing"
> (administering digitalis) while we were discussing all kinds of
> cardiotonics. I marked down that we should discuss that further,
> more thoroughly, and I'll ask the instructor to do so. Even on
> the floor, I'll take out my pad and say, "Be sure to discuss how
> this works, the mechanics of it."

Kathy takes notes mostly for review, but if they pose problems
in understanding, she will rewrite them so that they are easier to
understand.

> If it's something I really need to know, I'll go back and rewrite.
> For example, when I did drug classifications. We've had lectures
> on pharmacology, but I know I was really "stressed out" about
> this assignment, so I went home, reviewed and put everything
> into nice little categories. I could have either just collected all
> the data I had gotten from lectures or I could have fed back to
> her what she had given me, but I felt compelled to do this thing
> right, so I separated the overall category of cardiovascular drugs
> into five types and then chose the most important aspects that
> nurses should be concerned with, that is: what the drugs are
> indicated for, and how they work. I group things together a lot.
> I remember things better, and they seem more familiar to me
> when I can associate them with something.

She realizes the value of distancing herself from her material
and the forms she has written down — or up.

> I like to collect everything I need; for example, we have a lot
> of care plans to hand in. I like to have everything within reach.
> I number my books, then I note the necessary ones on a pad,
> so it's easier for me at the end. I write a lot of marginal notes
> in my books to refer back to or explain — so that I can under-
> stand what the book told me, put into my own words what's
> in the paragraph and hold it for ready reference. . . . I start out
> writing a great deal until I tire physically. Then I have to take
> a break and come back. I review what I had written. This proc-
> ess is repeated. When I'm done, I make revisions. Besides the
> grammar parts and stuff like that, I use priority-type things, re-
> arrange according to importance. If I think something is partic-
> ularly important, I stress it. If I have time I'll put it away and

come back to it. That certainly helps. It's amazing because you get so involved in something that you lose yourself, and you come back to it and say, "Have I really written that?"

Kathy classified a recent pharmacology assignment as a prototype of a helpful learning tool. Each student was given a drug classification and had to answer questions concerning his or her category: "How do drugs belonging to a group work? What are the nursing implications?" The format was flexible, with the questions acting merely as a framework. "I like that because you have something to go by, and yet you have the freedom to express yourself. Sometimes when you have a format or an outline that you have to follow, you're inhibited and then you lose out. I get agitated if I can't get it all in the format, and some of it goes by the wayside."

In addition to her writings in psychiatric nursing, she shared her notes and papers from her physical education course and her orthopedic nursing module. Interestingly, she approached each subject differently, using writing that she felt was specific to and appropriate for learning in each. The PE course dealt with weight control, nutrition, principles of cardiac physiology, musculature and its functions, and corrective exercise. Her class notes for this course reflect her sense of the factual character of the subject matter in their precise phrasing. Some of her strategies for learning through writing are manifested in the self-directed questions, marginal notes, and pivot words and phrases found in these notes.

Kathy's writing in orthopedic nursing concerned the rehabilitative therapy of several diabetics, each with a variety of complications: stroke, amputation, and hearing impairment. Here, her ongoing learning about both the technical and human dimensions of treating such people is evident in her writing. She maintains a careful balance between proper medical terminology — definitions/descriptions and comparison/contrast of symptoms — and her descriptions of the needs of each patient in the series of case histories.

Her writings in the psychiatric nursing module are the most comprehensive, however, covering a whole spectrum of writing tasks carried through multiple drafts. Through her effort in each draft, we can see her constructing her own knowledge. This sequence typically begins with brief, predicative notes on the orientation session, followed by highly personal bits of writing recording her first impressions at the mental health facility. These first day's clinical notes serve as source material for later writing and learning.

[First Draft]

MR is a 29 yr female who looks yonger than her age. She appeared clean & well cared for today. Clothes were neatly

pressed & make-up applied tactfully. Her initial reaction to me
[with]
was short, stating she had met c\ her Doctor today & would be
[with]
unable to spend time c\ me. But after a brief exchange of words,
she seemed to "warm-up" & become conversant. Reality orientation appeared good. She spoke often in retrospect of her illness
which brought her to TPH in May of last year.

[Second Draft]

1. Appearance — 29 yrs, looked younger, dress was appropriate &
   clean. Make-up was applied tactfully today.
2. Behavior — M smoked continuously thru-out the day. Movements were sometimes sporadic & quick — she constantly moved
   fingers or swung her foot. Eye contact was good.
3. Reality orientation appeared good. She spoke often in retrospect of her illness which brought her to TPH in 5/80. Logic
   was clear. no delusional or dissociative thought patterns observed.
4. Affect was depressed today, due to a missed Doctor's appt. She
   stated she felt "disappointed today."
5. Conversation was appropriate in content & timing. She did need
   motivation in starting conversation.
6. Physical — M did appear to have some anxiety type activity "pin
   rolling," swing foot. She had no somatic complaints.

The substantive change in the last sentence in the Daily Log is significant in that we can trace an attitude shift from the initial impression
to a personal conclusion that sets the tone for future learning about
MR.

Her next Daily Log entry describes the do's and don'ts of the
psychiatric interview; nursing personnel are taught never to ask
"why?" or to give biographical data. Instead, they are instructed
to ask "where, who, what, when, and how?" These guidelines lead
directly to written accounts, in a variety of modes, of all Kathy's
activities with her assigned patient. The sequence begins with a generalized narrative and goes on to a concrete, expanded list describing
the woman's appearance, behavior, reality orientation, affect, and
physical symptoms. These drafts and subsequent interactions in the
clinical area reflect Kathy extending her learning beyond her notes
through additional writing.

Here I realized that part of psychiatric nursing involved the
ability of being able to let people trust their own instincts to
what's right. I began to see how conditioned I had become to

do things for people, to know what was best for them and to
make sure they followed that advice. I realized how greatly a
psychiatric care plan differed from a med.-surg. plan. For example, a surgical care plan might read
a. Cough & Deep Breath of 2°
b. Ambulate bid
c. Force feed to 2000 cc per shift

While a psychiatric care plan is so individualized, made to fit
specific needs of a pt. MRK's care plan might look like this:
[with]
a. Explore problem solving options c\ her, but permit her to
   make her own decisions if they are reality based.
b. Listen to and positively reinforce MRK's attempts to talk
   about decisions involving life changes.
c. Be supportive of and praise all independent efforts.

With this in mind, maybe all my endeavors in nursing will be
truly patient-minded.

Instructor comment:
   this paper truly reflects your interest and concern for the
client's welfare —
   Good application of principles!
   mind the format of a research paper!

In addition to other interviews and interactions in the clinical
area, which show her following the same patterns of using writing to
organize her responses and learn from them, her Daily Log entries
cover two other kinds of experiences: visits to a juvenile correctional
facility and a unit for the criminally insane.

My day at Yardville Youth Reception Center was very interesting. I have always wondered where the "bad boys" in school
went and finally got to see it.
   I don't really know what I expected but was surprised to see
how things really were.
   First there were all the bars and keys for everything as we
took our tour. I was surprised to see all the work areas the boys
had a chance to get into and how clean everything was.
   After the concert (the boys attended) was over I got to speak
to the boys who were in because of homicide charges, I was ap-
prehensive at first but after seeing how mannered & well be-
haved they were I got more relaxed.
   You could tell they really enjoyed the company and they
asked all kinds of questions.
   I felt like I wanted to help them. I really came out with a
different attitude. I wish we could have spent more time there.

Later, when she reflected on this experience in one of the interviews, she remarked on the youthful offenders' attempts to convince visitors of their inherent goodness, saying, "Obviously, first impressions are of little value here. I think one would need time and a lot of exposure to 'the place' and 'the system' to formulate an opinion of what juvenile crime and its rehabilitation are all about." Putting her first impressions in writing seems to have helped her to move forward in her ability to see these young men and their behavior more clearly and realistically.

The culminating activity, the problem-solving paper, requires Kathy (and other students) to combine her interactions with her assigned patient in a format which accommodates patient/nurse dialogue and to enumerate the theoretical underpinnings and rationale of her work. To accomplish this synthesis, Raimondo asks four questions about results, prognosis, and identification of nursing needs to be answered in the paper. For Kathy, the last includes a statement of the patient's problem and of the complications caused by interference from the patient's aggressive friend. Kathy also reaches some significant conclusions through comparing and contrasting the respective missions of surgical and psychiatric nursing.

Interaction

Briefly describe the situation that led up to this interaction. "I met my client after preconference; we got her yarn and went into the day room to sit and talk."

Patient	Nurse	Comments
	Hi, my name is Maria, I'm a student nurse and will be here for the day.	*Giving information* — telling the client a little about myself to appear friendly and gain her trust.
Hi, I'm Verna.		
	What do you usually do all day when it's a holiday? Everything is cancelled isn't it?	*Giving broad opening* — trying to encourage the client to talk about herself and what she usually does but letting her pick the topic of conversation.
Oh, yea, it's boring around here on holi-		

Patient	Nurse	Comments
days. All the therapies are cancelled so we don't really have anything to do. I'm just going to sit and work on my afgan today.		
	You crochet? You'll have to show me your afgan. How long have you been crocheting?	*Offering self* in hopes of gaining her trust so she will talk more freely.
I just learned how a few months ago, this is my first one.		
	It's very nice, it looks great for a first project.	*Complimenting her talent* — encouraging client with her activity.
Oh, thank you, I'm making it for my bed, when I get married. I want it to be queen size.		
	When are you getting married?	*Offering general lead* — encouraging the client to go on about future plans.
On New Year's Eve, I am going to be married at midnight. I still have so much to do. That's why I have to hurry and leave. I have lots of things to arrange.		
	Uh, Huh.	*Silence* — waiting for client to expand on future plans. (After sitting and crocheting a minute, she began talking again.)

Patient	Nurse	Comments
Friday my son-in-law is coming and we're going to have a family meeting about when I'm getting out.		
	Oh, how long have you been here?	*Questioning* — want a direct answer from client.
About 3 months now.		
	How many children do you have?	
3 daughters, they are all married now. I also have my boyfriend, eh, fiancé. I didn't want to wear my engagement ring in here. It could get stolen.		
	Oh, does he live nearby?	*Exploring* — trying to encourage her to talk of her past, home, children and boyfriend more.
No, he lives in P–burg, that's where I am from. It's about two hours from here, up north.		
		Silence — for a few minutes she continues to work on her afgan. Finds a mistake and attributes it to not being able to talk and crochet at the same time.
I think I'm about ready to leave. They'll probably let me go in a couple of		

Patient	Nurse	Comments
weeks. I've got so much to do.		
	Yea, I guess so.	*Accepting* — giving indication of reception. Letting her know that I am listening and understand.
I've got to get a dress. Plan where to have it and get a minister. We want to be married at 12 midnight.		
	At midnight? Isn't that going to be kind of hard to arrange?	*Reflecting* — directing back to the client feelings & questions.
Well, maybe not at midnight. But definitely on New Year's Eve. We might have to go to a justice of the peace or something.		
	Yea, it might be kind of hard to find someone to marry you at midnight. Getting a justice of the peace might be the best idea.	*Restating* — repeating the main idea expressed.
		(Silence for a while; she continues to work on her afgan. Finally she starts to talk of nursing school.)
I'm an LPN, I have been one for about 20 yrs now. When I get out of here I want to start looking for a school to con-		*Offering self* — staying with client in hopes that she'll realize that I'm there for her to talk to.

Patient	Nurse	Comments
tinue my education. Eventually, I want to get a BS in nursing.		
	Really? Where do you want to go?	*Questioning* — want to see if client has really been thinking about this, or just made it up.
I'm not sure yet. Could you recommend someplace?		
	Not really. I don't know too much about the different schools.	
		(Direction of conversation has changed at this point.)
Oh, I guess I'll have to look around some.		
	Yes, that would be the best idea.	
		(Silence as she worked on her afgan some more.)
	Well, I have to be going now. It was nice talking to you. Bye.	
Bye, good luck in school. It was nice meeting you.		

1. *What was the purpose of this interaction? (That is, what were you trying to accomplish with your patient?)* "I was trying to get my client to open up to me. I wanted her to tell me about herself and her past. I wanted to find out how oriented to reality she really was. She needed to talk about herself and family so I could assess her. Visually assessing her was easy while we were talking. I wanted to watch her habits and facial expressions as she talked about different things. I wanted to see how close she was to recovery."

2. *Did your interaction accomplish the purpose you selected, and, if so, how; if not, why not?* "She talked freely but not really about the past. She seemed somewhat nervous but covered it well. She spoke only of the future which she seemed to fabricate as she went along. I found out she wasn't too close to going home. She had problems about where she was to live but wouldn't admit it. She acted as though everything was worked out already."

3. *What are your plans for the next interaction with your patient?* "I think she needs to talk further and needs to be redirected. She needs to be questioned more about her plans in hopes of bringing out the truth. She needed to relax more and give more trust in me as the interviewer. I would like her to open up more and talk more about her past life, not that she has three children."

4. *Identify the nursing care needs of your patient and suggest therapeutic intervention to meet these needs.* "She needs to be redirected to the reality of her situation. She should be asked specifically about her past but not unless you feel she is ready to talk about it or can talk about it, otherwise she could get frustrated and even regress. She has anxiety. Trying to get her to talk about her troubles and helping her to see the way to work them out could help her relieve this feeling. Frustration has got to be part of her problem. What she has set her sights on and what it seems like is going to happen are two different things. She needs to redirect herself."

The problem-solving paper received favorable comments from Raimondo because of Kathy's careful analysis, inferences, and conclusions. Thus, both Kathy and Raimondo see writing as playing a critical role in her learning in all the nursing modules. In psychiatry, writing aids Kathy in understanding and in making sense of things for herself. In the cardiac module, writing is important because there are definite things to understand.

You have to understand how the heart works; how the blood flows through the heart. Those things are established; everybody knows that, and nobody can argue it; whereas in psychiatry, you can say, "That's not the approach I would have used." I found it useful in the cardiac module to categorize types of medicines and kinds of people who were prone to heart disease. Here categorization played an especially big part because you could say, "This is the way the blood flows through the heart; in this abnormality the blood goes here, instead of where it should be going; this is the medicine that is prescribed for that." So you could see it when you wrote it out.

Writing enhances Kathy's on-site learning because the prospect of writing up her experience sharpens the way she pays attention, how she focuses in, and what she notices. "In psychiatry, we knew we had certain obligations. We had a problem-solving paper to write; we had so many interactions to do, and we looked for appropriate situations."

Beyond her clinical nursing modules, Kathy puts writing to use in many other contexts. She writes to understand numerical and quantitative concepts, to document subject matter, to classify, categorize, and reflect. Writing for academic purposes helps her make sense of things, draw inferences and reach conclusions, find similarities and differences, ask questions, and prepare for discussions. It enables her to pay closer attention, focus in more sharply, "tear material apart," synthesize, and reorganize. Kathy writes to achieve greater awareness and greater "in-depth knowing."

Myra's Writing

Myra is an intense young woman who, like Kathy, went to work right after high school. Her competence and hard work were soon recognized and rewarded by tasks and projects requiring increasing initiative and responsibility. However, Myra became restless and decided to enter the field of nursing. Upon completion of the A.A.S./ R.N. program, Myra plans to transfer to a four-year school for a B.S. in Nursing, as one of the requirements for becoming an independent, self-employed nurse practitioner.

Both her written work and her interview reflect unusual insight about her own learning process. Her orthopedics and pediatrics notes are highly technical and contain a number of illustrative diagrams. Her psychiatric writing is done in multiple drafts, with two much-annotated, handwritten sets of texts, followed by a preliminary draft and a typewritten final product. Even though she wrote the same interaction and problem-solving papers as her classmates, Myra's work showed more analytic and critical thinking skill. She also used unusual metaphors to focus her perceptions and her learning; about one patient she wrote, "his history was entwined with his delusions."

Myra makes self-inferences with relative ease: "I initially felt uneasy going into a locked unit; this was due to my not feeling totally confident in my abilities of successfully maintaining an interaction." She has other insights when she writes as well: "I felt the experience was valuable, not only to use my skills, but also as an 'eye-opener' for all of us. The bizarre behaviors and thoughts of

people actually happen and are not just 'stuff in books and films.'"
Myra also draws important conclusions through her writing: "The
experience stressed the need for skills of assessment, evaluation, and
insight in all areas of care. In this setting, a prison for youthful offenders, the lack of these skills could lead to dangerous situations."

When she took English composition, she wrote to learn how to
write, and when she first started coming to nursing school, she took
preparatory courses, such as biology and chemistry, to bring her up
to the same level as her peers. She knew that she didn't know how
to study, so she went out and bought a "How to" book. That gave
her study tools and, as a result, she always rewrites her lecture notes,
putting them in full-sentence form because that works best for her.
She also uses a personal outline as a learning tool. It is in these ways
that writing is "helpful" in learning.

Myra also wrote when she was a customer representative for a
computer firm. In order to explain the computer reports for someone else to understand, she sat down and wrote them in a sequence
that was understandable.

> I knew the reports, and I'd leave out something very essential.
> I had to learn to write from the perspective of someone who
> did not know what I knew. Something that would be very
> simple to me that I thought everyone knew, I had to come to
> realize they knew nothing about. I had to come from that posi-
> tion, even at the risk of insulting their intelligence. When I
> proofread and made corrections, I found that very useful be-
> cause it helped to crystallize how to explain to a co-worker
> how to do a certain study. I would sit down and write it out,
> so that I could verbally give it to them. I crystallized my own
> thinking, so I used it in my work and also in dealing with cli-
> ents all the time.

She began writing questions as part of training people to solve
computer problems. To create a learning situation, she would ask,
"What if Joe called and had this problem with the report, what
would you do?" And in training them to process what they would
have to do to find the answer, she posed situational questions, such
as, "What would you do if . . .?" requiring them to speculate and to
anticipate future events.

Myra also used writing as a major learning strategy in subjects
like anatomy. To understand the material, she made circles and
arrows, drew the system as she was learning it, and then wrote in
the information she wanted to remember. In nursing, she uses writing to outline chapters in textbooks and to remember material, often
coupled with drawing. At one time, she had entertained thoughts of

being an artist. It is part of her orientation, she thinks, to translate new information into something that she can draw as well as something she can write. It sinks in better for her when she uses the two symbol systems as aids to learning. "In nursing, and in most sciences that's possible. It was hard in microbiology because things are so small."

In discussing the types of writing she uses in her day-to-day functioning as a student and as a person, Myra remarked,

> In the psychiatric samples shared, I found writing a learning experience because they had a format that I needed to conform to, and so I had to organize my thoughts with those criteria in mind. I also had to organize my notes. I had to express myself within that format and organize my notes in a certain fashion, so that they would make sense later on when I put them into the format which is that one part in the final form. All my notes were taken so that the "client" side would be logically set up. That was the way I did it to have it organized for the final draft.

In several areas of study, Myra develops some sort of identification system. For certain modules, she puts tabs on workbooks so she can find the modules easily. That gives her an idea how much material there is, and she organizes her notes the same way, so that the lecture notes coincide with information for quizzes. She tabs corresponding pieces of information so that there is some kind of visual identification. For example, she knows that "X" number of pages covers the information for Quiz II. "I've done that with all of my notebooks. . . . I've had some sort of tab system so that I will know what's going on in them for ready reference."

Myra feels that this system of organization is permanent and will have practical applications for the future. She has gone back to notebooks from past courses, and since she has information on the front about when she took the course and also has it tabbed on the inside to find information, the search is simplified. She also tabs textbooks to match notebooks. For example, in anatomy she tabbed the skeletal system so that all the information was available for easy reference. "I use my notebooks as a library if I have to go back and find something."

Myra spoke about the social problems course which required essay exams. She was terrified of writing, but found that essays gave her some self-validation. She could assimilate the material from the lectures, films, and text and could put together essays which, though not completely polished, got the main points across.

. . . and so I found it a learning experience in a sense that I was better able to function in that area, better than I had thought, so I learned from that and each time that I had exams, I found that I could . . . my thoughts would become more crystallized, so the writing became easier instead of like pulling teeth. I learned in a sense that I can indeed do it. . . . A few years ago, when I was taking English I . . . and discussing with a friend how I was supposed to have an introduction, a body, and a conclusion, but I just jumped into the middle. We were talking about why it was I did that, and it was because I have difficulty beginning, overcoming a mental inertia to get momentum. That's why I wrote that way. I see that in retrospect I don't have that fear of starting something new now in my own life which is reflected in my writing. I am more able to begin now and not must have to jump in feet first. . . . I can indeed start the flow of something. . . .

She has a history of using personal writing to clarify her thoughts.

I used to maintain journals for years . . . just get a spiral note-book and start writing something . . . whatever came up. I haven't done that for a few years now. . . . I found it thera-peutic in that looking back on it gave me some insight into what was going on. I've been wanting to initiate it again.

Recently Myra did some research for personal purposes, i.e., for a friend with an ailment, and wrote it up. She found that interesting

because it was different than having to do it for school. It was fun; it was using all the textbook knowledge and experiences, pulling them together from several sources. It was fun because it wasn't required. I could play with it more, create my own structure and form and put in what I had thought. That was pleasureable.

She realized the potential of writing for learning when she first considered seriously becoming a full-time nursing student and mak-ing a commitment to overcoming her phobias about writing and math. Knowing that to achieve those goals she would have to "get her feet wet," Myra took some preparatory courses, and that's when she began learning how to study and saw that she needed to write. What worked best then were flashcards. In certain subjects they were just "invaluably wonderful," especially for chemistry symbols.

I thought if I could take something that I was learning in a text-book, or a film or a lecture, and I could take those notes which were in someone else's words and put them into my words, then I felt I understood it.

When she is studying textbook information related to other course material, Myra finds it helpful to take lecture notes, to let it jell for a while, and then to return to reading the textbook. Often, she takes down pertinent information, something she wants to remember, and puts it in her notebook so that three months hence, when an issue arises about a neurosis (or whatever), she can return to her notebook for a footnote reference or a bit of documentation.

She prefers written assignments that require her to think, for this means taking something she has learned in some area of study and not just "spitting it out," but "doing something with it." Her pediatrics group did that, answering questions like, "What problems would you face getting a two-year-old to take medicine?" Answers to such a question cannot be found in the textbook. The students, Myra felt, had to know what a two-year-old's reaction to medicine might be and what might be done so that the child would take the medicine without a problem. Such knowledge requires an imaginative synthesis of material learned from many sources. Myra commented, "I find this process frustrating but also helpful because I can use information I learned and put it together how I think it would work. Someone else may have the same situation, but her viewpoint may be entirely different."

Rote learning frustrates her even more, however, particularly when she senses that the instructor merely wants to weigh the finished product.

> I fail to see the purpose of just taking information from a printed page and putting it in my handwriting when I know that all they wanted to see was how well you could take it from there and put it here, and they don't care what you've learned from it or how to integrate it.

Writing, to Myra, has an important function in day-to-day living as well. When she has several jobs or errands to do, she puts them down in sequence. She also makes lists to compartmentalize activities. When she becomes a nurse practitioner, Myra plans to organize and prioritize tasks in order to avoid compromising her personal needs. When she was involved in the feminist movement, she used to write even the very informal talks she gave about women's health in which she presented information about basic anatomy and physiology. With what she knew of the subject and the audience in mind, Myra designed the informal talk and presentation.

> I had to design it, thinking of questions people would ask: from junior high teenagers to senior citizens. I constantly had to

question myself, "at this point, would someone think or would someone want to know about . . ." While I was writing the talk, I would have a skeletal written structure with adaptations for each group as well as for different situations. To organize my own thoughts, I had to write everything down.

The night before a clinical conference, nursing students are given a "client assignment" sheet which gives diagnostic information they have to know to deliver client care. They look up information relevant to that particular diagnosis and address such questions as: "What am I going to do?" and "How do I budget my time?" or "What would be important to know about this person's stage of growth and development in relation to the diagnosis?"

This goes for all areas including psychiatry, medical/surgical/ pediatrics, orthopedics . . . you will have to make preparations, and the diagnosis, see what implications that has. If someone is going to have a mastectomy, how is it going to affect their self-image? How will their body be affected because of their age group? I'd feel sort of stupid not having thought all of this out and written it out the night before.

This systematic approach to planning, using writing as a major basis, serves Myra well in both academic and professional work.

If I were doing client care, I would look up information in textbooks and write it down, taking notes; then compile an action plan depending upon needs, for example, social needs, safety, etc. From what I have read, done and experienced, I'd put together what I would do. There's prioritizing again: "What would I do to assure safety? What are the problems one day out of post-op? They're still groggy from sedation, so what am I going to do about it?" That's how I find out what things to do. . . . I use some sort of outlining in that. If I were doing a psychiatric paper, I would try to classify information. It helps to compartmentalize, to block things out and make some designations — all in writing.

Myra's sense of precision in describing her observations and of organization in thinking about and analyzing her experiences is evident in the writing she does in the psychiatric nursing module. She follows each assigned format carefully, yet she manages to come up with original, unfettered content. In a process recording she describes client needs and nursing interventions in separate columns. In the first, she has three categories: withdrawal, freedom from conflict, and personal appearance, each with a series of strategies designed to alleviate the problems.

Process Recording

3. Plans for another interaction would be to further dev trust & rapport. I would hope these would facilitate These would allow G. further opportunity to express himself and help dev establish goals.

4. ct needs

	Intervention
1. Withdrawn personality	1. foster cnt trust
	2. encourage group interaction c diff therapies
	3. establish one to one communi whenever poss
	4. be aware of several clues & evaluate and incorporate in interaction
	5. be sensitive to signs of withdrawal
	6. help establish goals ways to achieve goals
2. From conflict	1. help to resolve diff if @ all poss
	2. discuss diff in poss help resolve to overcome feelings
	3. contact social service for living job arrangement for discharge in light of family problems
3. Pers. appearance	1. encourage hygiene
	2. support his positive striving for improvement in appearance
	3. tie appearance c his goals for self support

Her interaction paper meshes narrative accounts of the session from both client's and nurse's points of view, preceded by a brief synopsis of the situation that generated the interaction and followed by a section in which she analyzes her behavior and its apparent effects on the client.

Interaction

G. joined me after the unit mtg and sat in the unit day room. Today was holiday so his therapies for the day were cancelled.

Client

1. G. appeared more cheerful and open than our first mtg. He greeted me, sat down and stated he bought some pointed out he had on his new clothes he recently bought. He seemed happy c them and smiled when I commented on them.
2. G. seemed eager to talk about his new clothes, he told me how many items he bought & the colors.
3. He had exhausted his completed his sharing and seemed interested in talking. He told me his wkly He talked about his therapies when asked. He enjoyed music therapy and had art therapy last Fri.

Nurse

1. I greeted G. and noticed his clothes were newer & diff than our first mtg. The fact that he first put out his clothes reinforced my hope that trust had been established. I replied the colors suited him.
2. I encouraged G. to talk, I wanted since he had initiated the topic I felt it important to follow his lead.
3. Since we had attended music therapy together, I asked his impression of the session. I hoped by linking our previous shared experience and other therapies, that he would cont sharing. He responded & talked about art therapy. I asked him what he does in art therapy.

Comment

1. I felt that my responding & sharing respect & being genuine on the previous visit had fostered trust. G. was very previously withdrawn and today he was willing to initiate & extend himself.
2. It seemed that G. had taken an interest in his appearance, and although his personal hygiene hadn't improved, I felt this was a positive sign.
3. I hoped by linking our previous shared therapy and his other therapy he would cont sharing. I also hoped this would allow him leads to other topics.

This interaction paper builds on an initial set of notes which were briefer and sketchier.

1. Appearance: clothes appeared clean but slightly worn, was not clean shaven, hair was short and seemed to need a trim. His gen hygiene practices seemed poor or neglected.
2. Behav: seemed shy c initial introduction but began talking more near the visit end. He also was maintaining eye contact for

longer time period. He "jiggled" rt leg when standing or both when sitting. Had twitch of rt side of mouth, tended to "wiggle" jaw. When smoking blew through clenched teeth.

3. thought and perception: did not reveal any gross disturb thought patterns or perception abilities. He wasn't able to maintain conversation of chain of thoughts for long period of time.

4. affect: He was generally quiet, withdrawn and seemed to be "inside himself"

5. communication: He answered question with brief answers but seldom carried the conversation on after answer. He would say a few sentences to expand his answer.

6. motivation: no observation

7. phys: appeared able to coordinate motor activities and navigations. No problems were demonstrated.

The sequence also led to an entry in the final version of her Daily Log.

Wed. Nov. 11 W9 Unit
The entire unit was involved in a meeting in the morning, which my class attended. G. met me after the meeting and we sat in the day room. G. appeared more interested and open today, he pointed out he bought and was wearing new clothes. Although he seemed proud of his new clothes and appearance, I noticed his personal hygiene was less than our first meeting. He talked about art therapy and that they were asked to write their goals. His were to 1) get well and 2) to get a job. He was more expressive today and told me what he meant by getting well, what he felt was wrong with him and asked help in figuring out how to job hunt. He seemed goal oriented, motivated and wanted to express his thoughts and ideas.

We went for a walk and when we returned to the unit, he seemed "talked out." I felt an attempt to continue talking might lead to increasing anxiety and cause him to withdraw. I felt a nonverbal activity might continue our contact without tension and anxiety. We joined a classmate and another client in a few games of ping pong. G. seemed relaxed to enjoy that level of interaction with others. I felt the focus change was beneficial, I wanted to end the day with G. feeling good about opening up to me. The game did not increase his anxiety and I felt he did not withdraw or decrease his trust.

Myra returns to this entire sequence of interactions with her client another time in her problem-solving paper. In this paper she distances herself a bit more from the events in order to generalize about this experience and its implications for "establishing and maintaining a therapeutic interaction." She elaborates on the difficulties in reaching a withdrawn, "one-answer" man and the intricate combination of intuition and training necessary for achieving therapeutic goals. She has learned, for example, that "the moment a person walks in through the door, she is giving personal information." Myra also pinpoints the challenge of interpreting behavior and acting upon her interpretation, something she seems able to do rather well. She is also able to reach the point, through going over this experience in writing several times and in a variety of forms, at which she can conclude that "sometimes cts are not willing & able to extend themselves and caregivers need to be sensitive & adaptable."

Prob Solv

Establishing & maintaining a therapeutic interaction c a new g can be diff. esp. for an inexperienced student. A prob. I encountered was with a severly withdrawn G. The staff has briefed me, G is a one answer man, he usually fades into the woodwork has no fam support & not to be upset if he abruptly leaves. I feel my skills of observation & communication were going to be greatly needed.

The staff found G & intro us in the breakfast room. I had a cup of coffee & asked G if he'd like one. He got coffee & sat down at the table. G was a very lg man & seemed uncomfortable c his appearance and skeptical abt himself. He chain drank his coffee and looked out the window. He had no eye contact but didn't seem ready to jump up & leave. I observed & evaluated G's actions, I learned infor which would help c communicate . . . the moment a g walks in the thru the door, he & she is giving personal info. People reveal themselves by posture, facial expression, gesture, movement and actions.

As I observed G, I felt he was uncomfortable but he was willing to "be there." He used to delay talking & I felt as if he was seeing testing to see if I was willing to "be there" also. I felt a little uncomfortable c the idea of initiating a conversation c a "one answer" person, but however I attempted to _____ verbal state I would stay.

G seemed to need a settle in phase & stopped his blocking after a few minutes. I asked re: his activities today hoping to lead to a discussion. His replies were brief, dance therapy @ 11 am, horticulture @ 1 pm. I asked open end questions re these areas. He only said they were OK. I cont c questions and he began to answer more than yes, no, & its ok. I feel the open ended quest tech was helpful c a diff _____. "an open ended question focuses on a topic yet allows for freedom of response." Wilson, p 170. The using this tech was less threatening to G. I felt using this tech was less threatening to B. I also allowed silence, coupled c silence was less threatening to G. If I cnt rapid fire questions, it would either drive him away or allow him an opportunity to express himself. I also used silence to convey I was making myself available.

G at one pnt abruptly got up and lef the room, I thought I'd done something wrong. I stayed setted remained seated, I noticed he'd left a lighted crgr & coffee, I interpreted this as he meant to return. G did return, he I learned he had gone to the rest room & staff felt he wasn't socially skilled enough to excuse himself.

G initiated 2 questions during our talk, he asked my full name & why the table centerpiece had been made (our class gave a centerpiece to gateway for the holidays). I felt his asking questions. . . .

I felt G was a challenge esp to my ability to observe interpret and act on my evaluation. G helped me to understand that making onself available, allowing silence and a sensa____ to & verb commune are needed in the import parts of communication. The experience also demonstrated that sometimes cts are not willing & able to extend themselves and that caregivers need to be sensitive & adaptable.

In her personal, working, and academic life, Myra has discovered some powerful writing strategies for planning and integrating material. Writing aids her efforts to remember, to understand, and to explain things to others. Note-taking from one source to prepare for study from another proves valuable as a means of learning. She writes to do things, to use knowledge in creative ways, and to solve problems. Writing creates a matrix for personal thinking and academic learning which is essential for her in conceptualizing, interpreting, and organizing her thoughts about her course activities. Furthermore, she recognizes the importance of incubation, as well as of multiple drafts, in thinking about and in clarifying material for later use. Myra asserts, and demonstrates, that writing and talking are interactive processes and can be used together in furthering personal and professional understanding and action.

Writing in Psychology of Human Relations

George Colnaghi has a way of achieving rapport with students at all levels of ability and accomplishment. His empathetic approach makes him a remarkably effective teacher. He is thoroughly convinced of the value of writing to think and learn, both for himself and for his students.

> I've come to this conviction over a number of years, both in my personal life and individual and couples' counseling; my classes, where I've tried out the technique; in workshops for specific groups. Consequently, there's nothing that I do now that doesn't include some writing. I find it just incredibly valuable to put it down on paper.

In his class, prior to our interview, one of Colnaghi's students was sharing something about his journal writing. He said it was wonderful to write in this journal because he could take these ideas that had been running around in his head, put them down on paper, and step back from them a little bit. Doing this take some of the emotion away, so he can look at the ideas clearly, and it "cleanses" him. There is a catharsis, and it "helps to clarify the thinking because I can see the circles I have been running in; I can't see them when they're in my head. . . ."

Colnaghi has seen this occur over and over again. "There isn't anyone I work with who doesn't have to write something, sooner or later, even it it's just making lists of what he wants and doesn't want." He elaborates:

> Having to write something for someone else forces me to think it through, where I ordinarily would not, as was the case in the counseling philosophy that I just had to write. I don't think I would ever have gotten down to thinking it out sufficiently to find out what my philosophy really was, had I not been required to put it down on paper. Having to think it out helped me clarify it to myself. While I can't say I need it to find out what I'm thinking, I find writing improves my thinking tremendously. For example, I may have an idea for a class. If it floats around in my head, and I just do it off the top of my head, three or four times during the week, say, with a number of discussion groups, by the end of the week, it's much cleaner. I can save a lot of time by just sitting down and "sketching" . . . it out on paper, and I find out that it's better right away.

Personally he has been using writing for learning for some time; however, he has thought of doing so in his teaching only recently. Nonetheless, he has developed and has been experimenting with several ideas. For example, he is beginning to use short bits of spontaneous in-class writing alone and in combination with small group discussions. Colnaghi does not consciously set out to strengthen specific course objectives by writing, but he maintains that in the course where he uses it most intensively, "Psychology of Human Relations," one main activity is having students take theoretical material and use it as a framework for examining their lives. Writing, he thinks, is essential to that process. "I would say that the overriding and overarching goal of the entire course is served most powerfully by writing. It forces the kind of personal introspection that can be reached only when you have to express yourself clearly on paper. You've just got to think it through."

According to Colnaghi, the most valuable written assignments in "Psychology of Human Relations" are those which result from a long writing process: free-writing that students are doing constantly in their journals and some directed writing together with list-making and letter-writing that are meant to open up, by degrees, the material that is to be brought together in that final paper. "Those papers get to be very powerful as a result of all the preliminary work that goes into them." Knowing they have that paper ahead of them, and that the small assignments are building toward it, makes students take the small assignments much more seriously. Everyone benefits from the careful sequence of writings.

When asked about feedback, Colnaghi says,

> It depends on the course, but in the one that I engage myself most in, "Psychology of Human Relations," I do two kinds of feedback. One is on their ideas. I share my thoughts, my feelings, and questions on what they've written, so that the papers become a personal dialogue between the student and myself. Then, in addition, I edit. I straighten out sentence structure, I circle, reorganize/rewrite paragraphs, tell them where it's vague. And I find that the papers improve in terms of structure, and the flow of language as the semester goes on.

Whenever possible, he photocopies all the papers, so that students can read each other's. However, he dispenses with the process if students are reluctant.

Often before the start of a discussion Colnaghi asks students to jot down their thoughts on paper. Some students take longer to get their thoughts together, and very often the discussion goes right past them, and they don't get a chance to express themselves. However, if they write, even in laundry-list fashion before the discussion begins, they are more likely to participate because they have their notes in front of them.

In all his teaching, Colnaghi is concerned that his students "develop skills for processing and applying information: knowing how to take information and do something with it." Student work, he finds, improves when students learn to ask the "What then?" question, or the "Well, what has this got to do with that?" question. It is in this "What then?" thinking that Colnaghi sees students shifting from giving responses in which he can recognize the book or hear his words coming back at him to giving responses in which he hears/reads them saying something unique or different. Often, what they say doesn't mesh with the angle that he has presented, but still it is unique, special. There is a palpable difference, he feels, when an individual is reconstructing knowledge rather than simply reproducing it. And, because he teaches with this end in mind, Colnaghi's students "gradually learn to speculate and to make connections."

To develop more ideal learning situations, Colnaghi schedules conferences with students who are astounded that they earned a "C" instead of an "A" on writing that had "all the facts." In the often tense interview that follows, they talk about "what's hard to talk about," i.e., that having all the facts is fine. However, a paper is above average only "when other things happen." Colnaghi strives to help students reach that stage by pointing the way with leading questions or with his own examples of how he would do it with that same information. Sometimes he will write a paragraph or two, or he will say, "This could be expanded and made more personal," or "this is something that I thought about; I'd like to see what you think about it." Thus, he provides models for further elaboration or investigation. At the end of a paper, Colnaghi may suggest to students that they look at the questions he has asked and ask those same questions of themselves. He gives them the opportunity to resubmit papers anytime they choose, with no penalty. Sometimes students take him up on this invitation, following his leading questions.

So, Colnaghi believes that writing can serve a variety of learning purposes, both for him and for his students. Writing can help in making choices and decisions and in constructing knowledge, especially in personalizing world knowledge to make it self-knowledge. It can be used to improve the quality of a new strategy, stimulate thinking, apply a theoretical framework to practical considerations, force introspection, paraphrase, summarize, analyze, and comment. Moreover, writing multiple drafts with audience feedback and/or teacher guidance promotes better thinking than producing a final product the first time. Also, because writing and talking are interactive processes, both benefit from sharing. While he is convinced that there is no one foolproof blueprint for effective teaching, he feels that carefully sequenced writing tasks do work well most of the time by gradually stimulating thought and learning. They also give greater validity to each piece of writing and, as a result, to the final product.

Sue's Writing

Sue's stamina and willpower pervade everything she does. A champion high school gymnast, she was told in her senior year that because of an injury she might never walk again, and certainly not without a limp. After a brief collapse, her feelings of despair turned to determination. Last year she not only walked but won many honors for her college swim team. Sue also is a licensed pilot about to graduate with an Associate in Science degree, and is in the process of seeking admission to the U.S. Air Force Academy. Her response when asked whether she used writing to learn was:

> I do it all the time: when I study, I don't just read it; I always write it down, maybe in outline form, and that will help me learn it. I've always done that; I have to physically put it down on paper, and it helps me learn. It kind of sets it clear in my mind.
>
> In physics, we have to write down the equations, and I found that making out a whole list, all the equations, just pulling them out of the whole chapter, all in order, I remember them better. If I have them all together, it makes it easier for me to understand, too.
>
> In something like English, of course you have to write, you have no choice in that. Outlines, I usually do mine before I finish. I can't outline before because I don't know what my thought process will follow. I basically write from what I have in my head, and I have to know about the subject to write. If I don't know anything about the subject, I can't write. . . .
>
> This psychology course is interesting because keeping the journal, I go back over what I had written and it kind of pulls things right back into perspective. Anything that sort of got blown out of proportion when I was in the middle of a situation: when I write it down and go back and read it over I say, "Oh, I was dumb. Why did I think that way? That was easy." The papers we write also help me put things into perspective. . . .

Sue makes lists "all over the place" of things to keep in order, of things to do because there are so many. She also makes a study schedule for final exam period. She puts down everything she has to do that day "to know what I have to do when. That's the best thing about writing: it brings things into perspective, and it gives you a sense of direction; it tells you which way you are going."

Often, she needs to write to know what she is thinking. Sometimes

> everything is in your mind and it's going 'round and 'round, and it's all confused and boggled, and you're in the same vicious cycle, and you can't make head nor tails of a situation. In the last paper I wrote in "Psychology of Human Relations," which was on relationships, I spoke about how my Mom just got a job in Europe, and I had very mixed feelings about this because she's going to be all the way over there, and I'm going to miss her like crazy but I'm really proud of her that she got this position, a very sought-after position, and I feel bad for not wanting her to go. I felt angry at myself: I wanted her to go and things were just going 'round in my mind. I felt like I had been dropped off a cliff, and Dr. Colnaghi suggested that that's what I write the paper on, and it was interesting because I started writing all these things down, and I said, "Now wait a minute. In order to understand what I'm feeling, I'll have to write down my relationship with my mom first." So, I did that. . . . Well, the paper was ten pages long . . . and I just went back and looked at it and said, "Wow, I really have a good relationship with my mom."
>
> Dr. Colnaghi used the example of his friend who was thinking of getting married and thought of all the good things . . . and then he thought of all the bad things, and decided he wasn't going to get married, and then he couldn't decide — it was so evenly balanced. But if he put them down, he could put them next to each other and weigh them. It really clears your mind out.

Sue also uses writing as a point of departure for new ways of thinking about herself and other things. For example, she was unaware of how much she had changed since high school until one night, when visiting her parents, she reread parts of her ninth-grade diary. She found that what she had written no longer had significance for her. In fact, it seemed to have been written about another person.

At this point, she plans to continue keeping a journal.

> . . . it clears my mind up. It's good for you. When you first write it down, it's like getting it off your shoulders. If you have a problem — I remember one night I came home and

I had a problem — and I just started writing, and it made me feel better.

Sue uses her class notes to help her prepare for tests.

A good example would be "Data Processing." I take notes during class of information that I feel is important, that the instructor seems to stress. Usually, I find it's helpful to write it out in longhand. Because if I leave it in shorthand I'll go back and say, "What did I mean by that?" If I abbreviate, later I use a key. I try to keep notes as organized as possible. . . . Usually, the things I write down are the ones I think I would forget. . . . If I write it down, I remember it; if I don't, I forget it.

If I find a misconception in my notes, I try to find the instructor and say, "This is what I've heard in class, and this is what the book says; now, which is right?"

Sue used writing extensively as a learning strategy in her aircraft components course. She did this because her instructor was a "good writer" and believed that every student should have good writing skills. She agrees.

To make it through life, you have to be able to write . . . so he made us write and answer essay questions. He checked notebooks. . . . We had one take-home test which was the major part of your grade. A lot of the tests were multiple-choice, but he'd throw in one essay question . . . just to make sure you knew the information.

The aerodynamics course . . . was the toughest because we had to write up labs. In addition to all the graphics and charts, we had to do a "purpose and explanation" of the experiment: why it worked or didn't.

In courses like physics and math, writing has helped her commit things to memory better than if she tried to memorize the information without writing.

I can put it on an index card and always carry it with me, and when I get bored, I can take the cards out and look at them wherever I am. . . . I don't have to carry the book around. The writing summarizes all the important aspects . . . and takes away the "garbage." It pulls out the most important points and from those points I can come up with all the other details.

And, in subjects like geography and aviation transportation, the required essays help her learn about certain things because she has to do research before she writes. To write the paper, she has to understand new material and form her own opinions about it, a process which she feels helps her grow.

Writing also helps her "research" herself, especially in "Psychology of Human Relations." There she has had to use writing to dig deep into her own personality. For example, she has been encouraged to think about her life goals. She began by wondering, "Do I really have a goal? Should I have one?" Having written these questions down, she lets her subconscious take over. "One of our projects was writing out our goals. I haven't really thought about them consciously, but last night, when we talked about them, I realized that I had been pushing harder to fly. . . . Writing clarified my goals."

Sue has found most helpful those thinking assignments in which the papers pushed her to expand herself, taught her something in which she was interested, and encouraged her to think back and find out more about herself in order to help her relate more to others.

She has known for some times that she remembered things better if she put them down on paper, and that it was a "royal pain in the neck" because it took her so much longer, but she also knew that she learned subject matter better that way. However, she didn't realize until recently how helpful writing can also be in clarifying her thinking. Some of her recent writing has started her thinking about the role of writing in thinking and learning.

> It's when my head begins spinning again that I realize I haven't been writing things down to clear my head. And when I'm most unorganized, I find I haven't written things down. Or I may have written them down, but I didn't check them over. But even then the material becomes more organized than if I hadn't written it down, because I still have a basic idea of what I have to do.

The hardest part for Sue, as for many of us, is getting started. Once her thought process is going, she finds it hard to concentrate on anything else. When she wrote papers for Colnaghi, she sometimes said, "I'm getting bored, I'll go do something else." But she kept returning to the paper in her mind and coming up with new ideas. Then, she would jot down these thoughts on a pad in order to get them out of her head. Otherwise, she couldn't concentrate on the new task she had begun.

Sue prefers journal writing to all other kinds. Because only she will read the entries, she doesn't have to worry about writing correctly. She usually does write in correct English, but sometimes her thoughts are so disjointed that she can be writing one thing down and thinking of something else. At those times, because she is writing in her journal, she often pursues the new thought rather than sticking doggedly to the original one.

If she is using a book with no review questions, she scans appropriate paragraphs, writes questions, and then tries to answer them. By doing this, she learns the material more fully and permanently. She also writes questions to prepare for other situations. For instance, she used this technique to prepare for her preadmission interview at the Air Force Academy.

> I just had to go before the Air Force Academy Review Board, and if I got in there cold, without having written out the possible questions and answers, I would have been lost. . . . On good advice, I wrote down a five-minute speech about myself. Writing it down puts it in your head with no need to memorize. Instead of groping for words, you find them right there. It took me a long time to write a five-minute speech, and I also prepared for five or six questions they were sure to ask and did. I started thinking about the answers . . . before the interview. I answered them in big words and little words, finding out what sounded best. It didn't sound as if I were reading them off a paper, but it sounded intelligent.

When questioned about her writing process, Sue said she writes her outlines last. Initially, she thinks and writes down basic topics. Then she writes the body paragraphs, which may take "a couple of drafts" because just as she completes the last paragraph, she may say, "I'd like to say something else up there."

Sue approaches the writing of a research paper by immersing herself in the research first. She takes notes on index cards and then carefully sorts them out. Though this is standard, recommended procedure, there is something physical in this process, as well as something that she can *see*, so what she ends up with from her point of view is something she knows rather than just pages of notes. This process works also because she puts things in words she understands. For example, she had just completed a paper on the destruction of the Hindenburg that consisted of a number of facts bound together by a great deal of personal speculation about them.

In "Psychology of Human Relations," Sue incorporated creative "seed sentences" into her journal writing as nuclei for her "Awareness" and "Emerging Self" papers. For example, she made a list of "Things I'd like to change about myself." These included:

> I talk too much.
> I need to care for myself more physically.
> I must concentrate better.

I should be more honest with myself and others.
I have to learn to control anger better.
I must stop procrastinating.

Later, she wrote a "truth about truth" list.

It can be painful.
It is a security blanket.
It is always best.
It can be complex, yet simple.
It can be a relief.
It is not always the easy way out.

For the "Awareness" paper, she turned again to making questions for herself to answer.

1. What zones am I in for the most part?
2. What happened when I purposely moved out to another zone?
3. Where was my awareness focused in each zone?
4. When my awareness is focused in one spot, what was I avoiding?
5. How has my awareness changed since taking this course?
6. What have I tried to change?
7. What would I like to change?
8. What do I focus on in my journal?

The journal entry on zones of awareness that follows these questions generates most of the thoughts and ideas which become the content of the "Awareness" paper. The paper portrays her excitement at this process of personal exploration and discovery. In it, Sue draws inferences about her feelings and thoughts and about their sources in her experience, and she makes new connections as she reconstructs her experience. She also enters the beginning stages of a new life planning process.

[Awareness]

I have been somewhat confused as to what is supposed to be written so I have decided to set this paper up as follows: at the beginning of each paragraph or series of paragraphs I will ask myself a question and try to answer that question directly in the following sentences. I have no idea about but I have the feeling the thought just entered my awareness that you may have been purposely vague in your instructions in order to see ~~watch sell see~~ what we come up with.

Throughout the past weeks I have been much more conscious of my zones of awareness, namely the outside, inside and mind zones, therefore my first question to myself is where ~~what zone~~

does my ~~thoughts~~ awareness continually go to and what happened when I tried pull it out of that zone into another? I have had a very difficult time with this question because my awareness seems to go to each zone pretty evenly. ~~My H If any~~ If I had to choose any the zone which to say I am in the most I guess would be my mind. It seems to be the easiest one to drift to and block out the outside world or pain w/in your body. I think the reason I am/would be more evened out when it comes to awareness is because of my hypoglycemia on my job. Because I am hypoglycemic I am constantly going w/in my body checking for any symptoms to try and catch them early. I have chosen to learn to do this to prevent myself from reverting back to the hypo more severe stage because they are pure hell to put it mildly. As for the outside zone my two jobs keep/help me in that zone because I deal with people. In order to do my job well I need to listen to people and really try to center my attention on ~~on~~ them. Also in flying you/I must constantly have my mind awareness focused on the plane (listening to it, and reacting to its movements) and on ~~the~~ everything outside the plane which could affect me, for example I should/ must react to clouds, storms, other planes, the air traffic controller, etc. I can not lapse into my mind or body or anything more than a min second or two or else I can become just another statistic. When I try to focus my awareness on something/ another zone I find it quite difficult to switch and keep my mind awareness there. One day, however, I was walking out to my car and I found my awareness to be in my mind zone. I quick opened my eyes (meant figuratively) and looked about me and I found that I was looking at a very beautiful campus. I noticed things which I had never noticed before.

Later, this journal entry, which is influenced in turn by the list of questions, is drawn upon in writing the following required paper.

The Emerging Self

Success, the one thing most people dream of, and yet, can never quite reach. If only they would turn around and realize how full their life is with their own personal successes. People always say "Learn from your failures," but did these same people ever realize how much they have to learn from their successes. I wrote down all the personal successes that I remember best, though there were numerous others. It feels good to look back and think on my life as small victories rather than a string of mistakes.

One personal success I remember from way back in the third grade was getting the highest score on the map reading test. It was one of those standardized tests which everyone had to take and when the test results came in, the teacher announced that I had the highest score out of everyone in our grade. I'm not quite sure what I learned from that other than the boost my ego needed because I was better then everyone else in at least one thing.

Some other personal successes I want to mention occured in my sixth grade year. The first was during our first gym class. We had to do the physical fitness testing. You know the one, when you have to do so many situps within a minute or so to attempt to attain the silver (About average on the fitness and coordination, can almost walk without hurting oneself), the gold (Kind of fit, almost able to walk and chew gum at the same time), the presidential (fabulous shape, ready for the Olympics, able to walk and chew gum with no problem and can even run no gum with the running) awards. There were about eight different tests the entire class had to do. One such test was the 600 yard run. Now none of us had ever done this before, so we weren't quite sure what to expect. We started off in a pack for our long journey of twice around the soccer field. After being kicked in the shins a couple of time, I thought to myself, "The hell with this, I'm getting out of here!" Once I lead the pack, no one ever got close to me again. In fact I lapped about a quarter of the class and turned in a record time.

About a month after this incident, soccer season started and being a little sixth grader I sat the bench alot. That is until the starting center half was injured and the second stringer was sick and I went in for the last half of the game and did a fantastically good job. After that, I was starting center half for the rest of that season and in the seventh and eighth grade seasons too. After both of these incidents I started realizing that I had a definite natural aptitude towards athletics. I also knew that I was above average in respect to athletics and that I should pursue it and take my gymnastic career more seriously. Also, I had a small peek at how I can handle pressure.

The third incident to occur in the sixth grade happened late in February. I caught a nearly fatal case of pneumonia. Within a couple of hours my temperature went from my normal 97.3° to 102°. By the time the doctor got there it was too late to move me to a hospital and my temperature was just one point under what theoretically the body can no longer function at. He did all he could for me, and then went about breaking it to my parents that I would not live through the night. By some miracle my temperature came down to about 101° that night and I was no longer delerious. I opened my eyes the next morning and said hello to the nurse and I swear I have never seen anyone jump so high in my entire life. The doctor later said that the only reason that I lived was because I was healthy, strong as an ox and my bodily endurance level was very high due to the fact that I was an athlete. I realized that I owed my life to gymnastics and being an athlete and everything my parents had every lectured me about athletics and how good it is to be in shape clicked into place. After that incident I became a fanatic about being in top shape. I still am to an extent a fitness freak, however not as radical now.

The next accomplishment that stands out in my mind happened in my freshman year. My very first highschool gynmastic season I received the Most valuable player trophy and placed third in the region in floor exercises, vaulting and all around. I realized from this that whatever I want bad enough, and I'm willing to work a bit to get, I can achieve. If I don't seem to be getting anywhere and I examine my motives, I will find that I probably don't want it bad enough.

During the second gymnastic season I had a number of accomplishments. The first one was at the Morristown High Meet. I had just worked out a new floor exercise to the music of "Hey Big Spender" and I was doing it for the first time. It was kind of a slinky routine to slinky type of music and of course opposite to all my previous routines (Wizard of Oz, My Fair Lady, Sweet Gypsy Rose). I always played to the audiences and then to the judges, in fact in a certain point in the routine I gave the audience a broad wink. The audience loved it. They were with me from the first shrug of my shoulders to the last flip of my head. They clapped and laughed and cheered for me as I went through my routine. The judges obviously liked it too because though it was a new routine which the kinks were not worked out of yet, I scored an 8.35. As a matter of fact, I never scored lower than an 8.35 the rest of the season. As for a message I got from this incident, other than boosting my ego, I guess when I think about it, it is "Give the people what they want and play up to them and they'll love you."

Another personal success during the season occured after the last meet against Dayton. After that meet we (the team) found ourselves the undefeated Conference champs. I was the last one on the bus and as I got on, the entire team started singing, "We love you, Susie. . . ." One of the girls got up and handed me a gift which was a gymnast on a balance beam. As she gave it to me, she gave a little speech that the team had made up. It went as follows;

> We want to thank you for leading the team to victory and keeping the team psyched up even though the odds seemed to be stacked against us. Thank you for setting a good example and for teaching us the true meaning of dedication!

I must have frowned or something then because she went on;

> Sue, you were injured during the last half of the season and even though you couldn't walk without pain, it never showed in your performance. You never showed anything except happiness in front of the judges and audiences and half the time in front of us too though we knew you had to be gritting your teeth in pain. Because you never complained none of us ever knew how bad it was until your sister told us that out of school you could not walk without a cane or crutches. It was an honor to work with such an outstanding gymnast, competitor, and person. We all hope that your injury is not serious and we will see you next year. Thank you for setting a good example. Good luck at the states and throughout your life.

I was so surprised and honored that I could not speak, Monica looked at me and said, "Don't say a word, you have already thanked us by your smile and tears." I thought the speech was a little much, because I did not live up to the standards in it, but it was a true honor to have my own peers saying this and thanking me. It took alot of guts on their part to come out and say this to me. Through this I realized (not until I was older) that you don't need to tell everyone how good you are or how hard you work or how you stuck to it even though . . . ! They are going to notice it and respect you for not saying anything. The saying "Laugh and the world laughs with you, cry and you cry alone" is so true. I only laughed when I was with the team and when I cried and gave in a little to the pain I tried to be alone. In the end when I guess they realized that like everyone else I did break down because I was starting to go crippled according to the doctor, and still put on a good face to the world. They admired me for that strength.

The week after that incident I went to the state championships. Much to my surprise I finally broke the nine barrier in vaulting. By nine barrier I mean, all season I had been scoring consistently 8.95 in vaulting. Finally at the state championships

I broke the barrier and scored a 9.25. Once you score a nine the judges and audiences get to know you and the scores will stay consistently in the nines.

I remember during my senior year in highschool, a friend, Jimmy and I were talking (at this point I had spent most of the remainder of my sophmore year and most of my junior year with a cane because I couldn't walk without it) and he asked me, "With all the bad things that happened to you in the past two years how do you get away from it all? I mean do you smoke cigarettes or pot or drink or take drugs or anything?" Without even thinking about it I said, "Jimmy, I don't get away from it. I just face it and live with it." Later I thought about what I had said and realized that if I could think positively like that regardless of all that had happened to me I was a whole lot better off then anyone else I knew. I realized that unconsciously I had taken the responsibilities and blows and eventually came out of it a whole lot better off than people twice my age. At that point my life started to change and it has been improving ever since. It was then that I realized that I was ready to join the human race again. I started to fight back and not accept the doctors verdict of partially but permanently crippled (I'd walk with a limp forever). Later that year I danced in a Musical and re-formed a dance club at my highschool. I still walked with pain but it was very slowly lessening. When I got to college the athletic trainer and I carefully rehabilitated my ankles. Now, there is virtually no pain in them at all. This showed me that, again, if you want something enough you must work for it and then it can be yours. Secondly I learned not to accept everything people say as the absolute truth. Accept all statements with even value, and find out more facts before accepting any statement as the truth.

In early November I was out on Lake Hopatcong racing Phantoms. One of the guys racing was the National Phantom Champion. In one of the races it was the two of us out in front with him slightly behind me. The wind shifted slightly and we both sensed it immediately and decided to come about. Now in racing there is a special come about called a roll-tack, where if done correctly the boat will actually gain speed rather than lose it. We went into our tacks at the same time and I happen to have hit all the conditions perfect and I came out of mine first. After he got everything under control he yelled to me, "Beautiful Tack, One of the best I've seen!" He had enough self-identity and confidence in himself that he could recognize and acknowledge that someone did something a little better than him. I admire that and try to be more like that.

In January, I started dating Todd. He was two years younger than me but the chemistry was right. The only problem was when I met his parents and they pronounced judgement on me. They decided that I was too old for him and that I would corrupt him (me corrupt him — I got news for them). After a month and a half of secretly dating I was to be the lead in a childrens play, which we did at various grammer schools throughout the area, one of them being Todd's father's school. I had worked with kids for five years and I figured anyone who was a principal had to love kids and they would probably figure anyone else who liked kids had to be an okay person. I have never worked so hard to get an audience with me and it worked. The next day Todd said that his father thought I was fantastic and wanted me to come to dinner. I had felt very uncomfortable and angry to have been judged before they knew me or even judged at all. It was a very frustrating feeling that taught me not to judge others in the same way.

I have had a number of successes in college. The first big one was my first solo in an airplane. It was proving not only to myself but also to all of those doubters who didn't think I could do it that I could, and I did. It was one of the biggest thrills in my flying career. I feel that it reinforced the theory that I cannot take what others say to be true until I have more facts and I can do whatever I set my mind to.

Later my freshman year at Mercer, I competed in the Swimming and Diving Regional Championships for one meter diving. I had never dove before in my life except for the month and a half just prior to this meet. I wanted to make a comeback in athletic competition and I was scared to death that I would fail miserably. I had caught a nasty cold about a month and a half before and it had been hanging on all season. However, my old determination came through and I competed anyway. My energy coming from a bottle of chewable vitamin c, somehow, I walked away with second place of the women and third place overall and also totally amazed people because I had only been diving for a month and a half. My second year diving I won the women's division for both one and three meter and made the women's All Region 1st Team. At the Nationals I took third on high board and fourth on low board and became an All American. Just the fact that I competed in the Nationals was enough. Again as in the first year I was going against the odds. I aggravated the condition which I didn't know that I had. As a result I was pulled from competition for three weeks. I was finally aloud back up on the board just five days before the Regionals, and just ten days before the Nationals. I refused to give up and as a result did better than I had ever dreamed of doing. The moral: You can do anything you set out to do as long as you work for it.

The last and most important personal victory to me is how I have changed within the past couple of years. I am a much mellower person (believe it or not) and able to better handle interactions with others. Most important I have started to roll with the punches much easier. Last January, I found out that I am hypoglycemic which is a condition that could kill my career as a pilot. I accepted it, found out what to do to treat it and then went on with life. I have got to admit I was somewhat upset and depressed when I found out the full implications of the illness, but I wasn't devastated by it like I would have been a couple years ago. When I had to "retire" from gymnastics because I'm "lame," I basically dropped out of life and closed myself into a shell. I don't do this anymore because I can't. I have changed too much and become more balanced. By this I mean, I am not at one end or the other of a spectrum of emotions, beliefs, habits, personality and such. When I was a gymnast I was the most conceited, daughter of a bastard you ever could have seen. Now (I hope) I'm not like that anymore. If anything I don't have enough confidence in what I do. I try to be unique in what I do and I dress and eat what I like and just do things I want to do. I'm not a total non-conformist because I won't go out of my way to be different. If I happen to do something that conforms with the norm, that's nice. I am proud of the fact that I can do my own thing without always feeling pressured into conforming. I call it uniqueness, others call it being a radical. Oh well, that is their problem, By the way I also try not to hold to much store by what others say where I used to believe everything people said.

As I wrote this paper I found that the majority of my victories have to do with athletics and competitions. I feel this is because my parents brought me up to be very athletically minded. I also had alot of trouble writing this paper and I don't feel that it is as good as my first one. Many of the lessons learned were not realized till very much later in life so my experiance of them is much broader than it actually was at the time. All in all, I found this assignment very enlightening with regard to my own view of myself.

Sue writes for a wide variety of learning purposes. The flashcards she makes help her to summarize and memorize material. The questions she develops assist her in preparing for various test situations. She also writes to identify the essence of a subject and to gain perspective on it. Writing thus helps her enhance her understanding, and it helps her in locating, analyzing, and solving problems. Further, she uses writing to make value judgments, to improve her sense of self-worth, and to obtain emotional release. This is particularly true for her journal writing, which she sees as very important for her. She gives us a profile of a determined young woman who not only sees the value of writing but uses it actively and variously.

Sandra's Writing

Sandra, who is married and has young children, was trained in accounting and works part time in that capacity at the college. She takes courses that interest her intellectually or fulfill an emotional need. "Psychology of Human Relations" did both.

She uses writing for learning in every course. One major avenue is note-taking followed by subsequent reorganization of the notes to engage further with the material. The process of rewriting her notes seems to embed things in her mind.

In the psychology course I'm taking now, I've learned most about myself by writing my feelings, my thoughts, things I had never done before. For another instance I'll use an auditing course I took last year. Most of it is theory. Then there are questions at the end of the chapter. For me to relate them to something I have only read and give answers is not enough. I have to go back and put the theory into my own words. I seem to be able to learn better that way. That's separate from class notes. . . . In class, I write about what the teacher says. And I later rewrite these notes. I remember them if I do them again. . . .

I was so perturbed about having to do so much writing in this course that I almost dropped [it]. Then I realized that I knew when I chose to take the course that this was an area I needed work in. Now I find myself writing more. If I'm having a problem in a certain area, or I'm having a problem about having a thought about something that I can't get clear in my head, I'm confused about something, I'll start writing some things down about it. It doesn't always clear it all up, but often it does.

Sandra can best exemplify the idea of helpful assignments by referring to "Psychology of Human Relations" because that is where students do a journal, on-the-spot writings, and longer papers. Of all these, she finds the in-class writing most helpful. Colnaghi gives "seed sentences" such as "I think . . ." and students put down their thoughts.

You just let them go when you think them, they're very fast, and you don't pay too much attention to them. You put them down on paper and you have to go back and look at them. Then you have more time to think about and analyze them. Makes more of an impression. Then you really give it more thought in one area. When you come back, you can expand on it because it's there to remind you.

She always understood that writing things down helped her to memorize them, but she realized only recently that writing things down can help her understand them.

I just never did it before. I always wrote to study for tests and knew that from writing, the subject ingrained itself more on/in my mind. But how I feel about writing now goes beyond book things, class subjects. Now I can use it on a more personal level to find out more about myself. I can look back at what I wrote three months ago and compare it with what I write now and see the growth in myself, a change in my feelings and my attitude toward things. I can see an honesty in what I'm writing, whereas when I talk to someone I don't always say the things I want to say.

Commenting on the possible future uses of the writing to learn strategies she is developing now, Sandra says, "As far as getting my head on straight, I'd like to continue. Now it's like an assignment. Sometimes when you don't have to, you sort of get away from it. But the truth is now, every time I have a few minutes, I'll get my book and write down a few things. Or if I have a problem, I say: 'Let's write about it and see what it looks like.'"

Sandra is most comfortable writing on her own time, for her own reasons, when she is the only reader. She is least comfortable writing a paper for someone else to read. As a result, when she writes for someone else, she makes several starts and ends up feeling "uncomfortable." In her job, she writes down a lot of questions. If she doesn't know how to handle a certain thing, she becomes nervous and fills her calendar with questions. In addition to the questions, she makes lists and writes reminders to herself and others.

Sandra also likes to use writing to prepare for discussions. When she does so, she feels as if she can be more direct and honest than if she hadn't undertaken this particular kind of preparation. Often, she feels as if she knows exactly what she wants to say.

When she writes a paper, she usually does it two or three times before it's finished. She starts by putting down thoughts in rough form. Typically, she doesn't like the way she says things the first time. To achieve the desired effect, she adds words and sentences as well as rearranging sentences to get her ideas across more clearly. Thus, she has come to appreciate the value of multiple drafts.

It's a thinking process, and as I'm wording it, sometimes I'll write a sentence and change it in the middle because that's not how I wanted it to sound. One example may be the paper I was writing on "Relationships." I was referring to my mother and I said that she wouldn't understand something in my life because she was older, and I changed it to something more accurate, to say I didn't think my mother could understand because she lived her life in a different time. Things have changed so much since, that she could not understand the things I was thinking and feeling and wanting to do.

Like all her classmates in "Psychology of Human Relations," Sandra wrote in a journal to evolve a process of values clarification and pursue the goal of learning about herself. The journal also became a rich source of material for the "Awareness" and "Emerging Self" papers. Each of these writings plays an important role in Sandra's process of developing self-knowledge.

Awareness

I used to think that I was an *aware* person. In the last two weeks I have come to realize that, yes, I have been aware of many things, mostly external, but totally unaware of far more.

Just sitting quietly and letting my mind become conscious of what my body is doing and feeling is a small revelation in itself. I've always been a busy person with a really hectic schedule. I never thought to take ten minutes to just recognize and acknowledge my own life signs like listening to my breathing and feeling it move through my body. And feeling my heart beating. Everyone has felt their heart pound during stressful or exciting times, but how many of us are aware of it beating at quiet times when it's not demanding our attention.

I have spent so much time inside my head and missed so much happening around me and inside me. I have spent too much time thinking and not enough time being actually aware of how I feel about outside events and how my thoughts make me feel. Now I'm beginning to take the time to savor these feelings.

Of course, to some extent I was aware of how I felt but now I say to myself, "I am feeling this feeling because I am thinking this thought or seeing this thing or hearing this sound."

Last week in class, I had the experience of realizing that when a certain thought entered my mind, I tensed up. I'm sure that I experienced that feeling before but I never really linked everything together and acknowledged that I was tensing up because this thought was stressful for me. Now, with this awareness, I can take this thought and analyze it and find out why it is stressful. Maybe I can do something to alleviate this stress.

Last week I did something for someone in my division. He took the time and went to the trouble to send me a thank you card. When I opened the card and read what he had written, I was aware of an overwhelmingly good feeling coming over me. Ordinarily I would have thought, "Wasn't that nice of Fred?" and not even thought of how I felt inside. Taking the time to allow myself to feel good made the good feeling seem even better.

After two weeks of focusing my awareness on my feelings (which is the part of me that I have been burying for a long time), it was surprising to acknowledge this really good feeling inside and know it was there, not just dismiss the act as something nice that someone did.

Looking further inside, I experience a feeling of fear. By acknowledging the fact that certain thoughts which I mentioned before make me very uncomfortable, I feel that unless I do something about who or what is causing these thoughts, my life is not going to be as satisfying for me as I might want it to be. Unfortunately, doing something might cause a very big upheaval in my life . . . and I don't know if I'm prepared for that yet.

Being aware isn't always enjoyable or easy to face.

This paper, both as a process and a product, grows naturally into one entitled "The Emerging Self," an articulation of new feelings and concepts about the self and others.

The Emerging Self

My earliest memories of success are wrapped up in the memory of my father. He loved all of his children but his sons held a special place with him. Because I wanted to be allowed into that special place, I imitated everything my brothers did and successfully impressed my father with my tomboyish ways. I played football, basketball and baseball with the boys on the block, went fishing with my Dad and brothers and cleaned the fish I caught. I even ate the same food he ate; things my brothers wouldn't touch. I went sledding down the steepest hills, learned how to swim before age five and dove off the bridges with my older brothers at the swimming holes. I spent most of my summers at the city pool and started to swim competitively when

I was eight years old. I remember how important I felt when my father came to watch me race and I won.

I guess at the same time my femininity was struggling to be recognized because I became involved with learning the feminine art of water ballet and performed for three years in the water shows at the city pool.

During my grammar school years I tried out for and made the chorus and was chosen to play leading roles in most of the school productions.

In junior high school I started noticing boys in a different way and I was very pleased when they showed a mutual interest in me. Also, making the honor roll for the first time at that time was almost like earning a Ph.D.

After high school, I went on my first formal job interview and almost died from nervousness but all went well and I landed the job.

After I got married, I surprised myself by becoming a pretty good cook. Surprising because I never showed any interest when my mother tried to teach me. Although my father played a very important role in my early development, my mother is the one that I most naturally emulate. I share my mother's love for cooking and appreciation of nice things, like lace tablecovers and fine china. When I'm successful at tastefully decorating a room or having a dinner party, I owe that to my mother. She is a very talented lady.

One of my most recent successes has been returning to school. Not an easy thing to do after taking so many years off to raise a family, and yet far more enjoyable and challenging than I ever remembered school being before.

Competing with my brothers for my father's attention and gaining it gave me a sense of self-confidence that I've carried through the years. I've never felt that there was anything I couldn't do competently if I really put my mind to it. From competing in sports against the opposite sex who were supposedly more athletically inclined, to trying out for school plays, to proving I had competent mental capabilities, every success built up my feelings of self-worth and equality.

The equality part didn't come easy. (The believing did, but not the proving.) I've always felt, even as a child, that females were at least equal to males in most areas and should have the same rights and privileges. I have met with much opposition to this idea, first from my parents and for the last 20 years, from my husband. Although he has been supportive in some of the things I want to do, he has many double standards.

As many problems as this opposing point of view has caused me, I am still determined to reach out for the personal goals I would like to achieve and the rights I feel I am entitled to.

The most important goal to me at this time is to develop a closer, more understanding relationship with my children. I would like to continue going to school even after I earn my degree in accounting from Mercer County. I would also like to work on my relationship with my husband. Even though he says he supports me in my decision to continue my education and hold down a job that is interesting and challenging to me, there are many times when I feel his displeasure because I'm not at home as much as he would like me to be.

Something else I have wanted to do for years is to take music lessons. I've wanted to play the piano ever since I was a little girl and my parents couldn't afford music lessons for both my brother and me.

Time seems to move so swiftly, I feel that I have to do as much as I can while I am still able to. I realize that doing the things I want to do takes me away from my family much of the time but I feel that after spending a lot of years devoting myself to raising a family and considering their desires and needs first, that now it's my turn.

This paper on "The Emerging Self" is, in turn, a source for a subsequent paper, "Closing the Gap." In the first draft of "Closing the Gap," Sandra inspects and begins to think critically about her relationship with her daughter and her mother. In fact, there seems to have been a useful cycle established from the journal, to the paper on "Awareness," to the paper on "The Emerging Self," to the paper on "Closing the Gap." Each in its own way has given Sandra a way to move both her thinking and her understanding forward.

Closing the Gap [First Draft]

I have been working on two relations in the past/last month. The one is with my oldest daughter and the other is with my mother.

Somewhere

My daughter and I were very close when she was a little girl. As she grew into a teenager we lost that closeness. She became closer to her girlfriends and confided in them. I continued to treet her like a child and failed to recognize that she was becoming a young adult. She changed/became very developed into a rebellious being and I became very domineering.

It's taken a long time for me to realize/accept her as a young responsible young lady. (She certainly has a lot of maturing to do but the signs so far are encouraging.)

What has helped our relationship the most is the ~~are the same times is the~~ fact that we can sit down and talk to each other. I've taken the time to sit back and look at her and I became aware of listen to her. Most of what I see and hear I like. I don't approve of everything she does but I know I have to give her space to make her own decisions, and learn from mistakes that hopefully are not too serious. I can't live her life for her. All I can do is be there for her when she needs me.

My relationship with my mother has grown recently. She's been ill for the last year and I've spent more time with her. but it's only been lately that we've developed a closeness and for me an ability to confide in her like I didn't do before. I always thought my mother was too critical of me but in the last couple of months I've received more support from her than I thought I ever would. She still tells me when she thinks I'm wrong (I guess all mothers always will) but when I open up to her and tell her things that I know are hard for her to accept she responds with kindness and understanding and support.

There are many things I thought I couldn't talk to my mother about. Because she was older and set in her ways I didn't think she would understand the feelings I had about marriage and career and life in general. But gradually I've covered almost all of these subjects and found that she accepts how I feel even though she may not ~~fel those~~ have the feelings herself think along the same line that I do.

There is still a barrier in my relationship with my mother. As much as I have confided in her, I feel she is holding back something from me.

The changes from the first draft to the second are subtle rather than sweeping. Nonetheless, we can see her using the thinking and the language of the first draft as a basis for fine-tuning her initial analysis of these two crucial relationships. At the end of the second draft, we are left with the feeling that, through the writing of this paper, she has moved forward in her pursuit of a fuller understanding of these relationships and of what she might (and might not) be able to do about them at this point in each of their lives.

Closing the Gap [Second Draft]

I have been working on two relationships. One is with my oldest daughter and the other is with my mother.

My daughter and I were very close when she was a little girl. As she grew in to a teenager we lost that closeness. She became closer to her girlfriends and confided in them. I continued to treat her as a child and failed to realize that she was becoming a young adult. She became very rebellious and I became very domineering.

It's taken a long time for me to accept her as a responsible young lady. She has a lot of maturing to do but the signs so far are encouraging.

What has helped our relationship the most is the fact that we can now sit down and talk to each other. I've taken the time to sit back and look at her and listen to her. Most of what I see and hear I like. I don't approve of everything she does but I know I have to give her space to make her own decisions and learn from mistakes that hopefully are not too serious. I can't live her life for her, all I can do is be there for her when she needs me.

My relationship with my mother has grown much richer in the last year. She's been ill for that long and I'm spending more time with her. But it's only been in the last 2 months that I've opened up to her and confided in her ~~like~~ which I didn't do before. We've developed a closeness I didn't think possible because we're very different from each other and I never thought she would understand some of the things I felt and some of the things I believed.

I always thought my mother was critical of me but ~~in the last couple~~ recently I've received more support from her than I ever thought I would. She still tells me when she thinks I'm wrong (I guess all mothers always will), but when I tell her things that I know she doesn't understand about and that are hard for her to accept she responds with kindness and understanding and support. This encourages me to talk to her even more.

There were many things I thought I couldn't talk to my mother about. Because she lived most of her life in a time when women played such different roles, I didn't think she could understand the feelings I had about marriage and career and continuing education. Gradually, I've covered almost all of these subjects and found that she accepts how I feel even though she may not think along the same lines as I do.

There is still a barrier in my relationship with my mother. As much as I have confided in her, I feel she is holding back something from me. My mother has been very nervous and depressed for a long time now and when I try to talk to her about it, she says she doesn't know why she feels this way. I think she has a fear of dying or of becoming very sick, but she won't tell me. I don't think she even admits it to herself. I hope that if she ever does decide to talk to me about it, I'll be able to handle it.

Through this series of writings, Sandra carries out the intellectual operations of analysis, reflection, and synthesis. She reconstructs, and thus clarifies, her understanding of the evolution of her relationship with her daughter and mother. Perhaps, in the next writing that she does on this topic, she will begin to see how the pattern of her relationship with her mother is being repeated in her relationship with her daughter. And, if this happens, perhaps she will be able to break the pattern and create a new one that is more to her satisfaction.

In sum, Sandra writes both to find out what she is thinking and to revise that thinking as a result of the insights gained from the writing and from her reflection on the writing. In some courses, she writes to learn course content; in others, like "Psychology of Human Relations," she writes to learn about herself. In both, she realizes the learning value of putting things in her own language. She has truly discovered the power that writing has for personal growth and for academic and professional problem-solving. She has gained an intellectual and emotional tool which will be available to her throughout the rest of her life. As another student in "Psychology of Human Relations" said, "Writing in this course helps me take other people's words and filter them through my mind."

Writing in Psychology of Women

Angela McGlynn uses writing personally and professionally in several ways; she writes letters to friends who live far away, as well as to her husband, "who lives with me." She writes out her lectures and other notes. She also writes for magazine publication and has had a book, written in collaboration with a colleague, published. McGlynn also writes lists. She writes for personal purposes when she is upset and when she is happy. She has a personal journal and looks back often to see where she was six months ago and how far she has come.

McGlynn believes that writing and thinking are so intricately intertwined that they are almost impossible to separate. In her view, writing clarifies thought; it helps us analyze situations, reach conclusions, and search for alternatives. She maintains that we often don't know what is inside of us until we write it down. In addition to lecture notes or data, she writes herself special notes for class and has been using "writing to learn" strategies knowingly for about three years. But she has used them unknowingly for ten years — as long as she has been teaching. She got started because she realized how important writing had been to her as a student: how it had helped her think about concepts and ideas. Many of her course objectives that ask students to define, describe, specify, classify, compare, contrast, and analyze are activities strengthened by and best done in writing. Through the years, McGlynn has developed a sense of what works. For example, she finds the reaction papers she assigns consistently most effective. They force students to choose a topic they would like to know more about and find three magazine articles that deal with their subject. They must read, take notes, think the problem through, and integrate the information in a three- to five-page paper.

The writing component of her courses increases students' problem-solving ability by requiring that they research, analyze and comment on situations, take a stand on controversial issues, and justify and support their position based on evidence.

I can recall individual student papers that offer evidence of having worked through academic problems.

I have also been using some of the brainstorming ideas of the Committee on Writing Across the Disciplines, having thought about them to figure out how they fit into my discipline.

McGlynn uses writing to complement other classroom activities by asking students to prepare for discussion in writing (giving individual views and/or group consensus). She also has students write on-the-spot film critiques. The feedback she gives to students is varied. She edits their work for poor organization and makes marginal comments showing enthusiasm or anger and finding fault with generalizations. Comments may be in the form of "this is terrific" or "you are making (a) statement(s) not borne out by research" or "don't jump to conclusions," etc. At the end of the paper, she gives an overall response to the subject matter, suggestions for improvement, and, sometimes, words of caution about using someone else's ideas without acknowledging the source. Her papers are graded in final draft form — she does give completely non-evaluative comment (written feedback) on extra-credit student writing. "Feedback is almost always immediate because I know how concerned I used to be as a student about the results of my efforts." McGlynn is also interested in student feedback and makes special provisions for comment on their written assignments or her end-of-semester evaluations. Subsequently, she modifies some of the writing strategies on the basis of student feedback.

McGlynn defines learning as a change in behavior resulting from knowing how to do something new. She comments further that learning has cognitive (intellectual) components which change the knower. However, to her, learning occurs in behavioral terms when a person is aware of something or can do something that she was not aware of or could not do before. As for her own awareness of the role of writing in thinking, she remarks that she was always aware of the value of writing in thinking and learning. However, she also recognizes its value in providing flash insights and considers it invaluable for varied academic purposes, as well as for personal and intellectual problem-solving. Through her empathetic treatment of students and her obvious concern for their learning, McGlynn transfers her regard for writing as an effective learning tool to her students.

Evelyn's Writing

Evelyn returned to school after a 10-year interval following high school graduation, ready to make the most of her new, highly valued college education. While her devotion to a five-year-old son is quite evident in the schedule adjustments she makes to be with him, her commitment to higher education is strong enough for her to contemplate pursuing a Ph.D. in clinical psychology. Evelyn is exceptionally capable and diligent, equally talented in mathematical and verbal areas. As a matter of fact, her fascination with the logic and precision inherent in mathematics helps her greatly in the humanities.

Evelyn has shared her writing from "Sociology" and "Educational Psychology" as well as "Psychology of Women." She indicated that she has probably used writing more in 1981–82 than in any prior year.

> This year, in college, I have been using writing to learn in psychology and in mathematics class; most especially, in psychology, by making flashcards to help me learn; just writing information down is a help to me. Then in mathematics class, any kind of mathematics, you just write it down and figure it out over and over again.

Evelyn explained that her writing efforts were directly proportional to the degree of enthusiasm. The excitement generated by her interest in the study of psychology and the suspense created by her viewing mathematics as a series of fascinating puzzles spurred her on to writing and to learning. "For both mathematics and psychology, there are concepts and information that have to be learned and recalled very easily or rather that I want to be able to recall very easily," Evelyn concluded. In psychology, a great deal of her writing consisted of interpreting material she was reading: magazines, books, films she saw and workbooks she used. She would arrive at her own interpretation of the material, put it in her own words, and write, as in the following:

> ### Femininity-achievement incompatibility.
>
> In adolescence, culture states to a female that achievement and femininity are incompatible — that is to achieve is not gender appropriate. A girl who achieves and continues to do so is unfeminine. To be feminine then is to not achieve. Important values these are in conflict.
>
> Achieving & on the form of getting good grades are encouraged up to adolescence when emphasis shifts suddenly to conforming gender-role expectations. A females desire to be appropriately feminine. Society at large does not value the female role! (So how come this female conforms then? The pressure is enormous. It must be worse to be non-feminine. I think females are brainwashed to be helpless.) (Why does the female not see an advantage in being a non-fem achiever than a fem non-achiever? It has to be of crucial importance to be gender appropriate!)
>
> It looks like, then, that in spite of the low value placed on the female role, it is still
>
> Probably the single most important influence on female personality lies in the conflict between achievement and femininity (Horner 870, A, 1972). The adolescent girl is caught in a double-

bind situation in which she wants both of the 2 alternatives but the 2 alternatives are seen as incompatible. In this are the origins of much of the ambivalence and conflict in female personality: the adolescent girl finds it hard to combine because of imposed cultural contingencies being a worthwhile individual and a proper female. (Boverman et al 1972) This is a source of adjustment problems for adult women.

Patient and Patriarch:
Some of the general issues discussed in this chapter are (1) Why are more women involved, so voluntarily or involuntarily with mental health professionals than men are? (2) What are the American psychotherapists views about women. (3) What practical implication does do these findings have for women who are in a psychotherapeutic relationship.

1. A study published in 1970 by US Dept of Health indicates that, in both black & white populations significantly more women than men reported having suffered nervous breakdowns, psychological distress, dizziness, nervousness, insomnia, trembling hands, nightmares, fainting and headaches.

   A study published in 1965 reported more that women patients outnumbered men patients 3 to 2 in private psychiatric treatment. Other ~~studies~~ data from studies support that women seek profession help for mental problems concerns more than men do.

   Private psychotherapy, like nursing, is an integral part of middle class female structure.

   It may be that more women than men are envolved in psychotherapy because it and marriage are socially approved institutions for middle-class women. Psychotherapy may be used by many women to keep a bad marriage together or as a way of ending it to form another marriage. Some women may use psychotherapy as a way of learning how to catch a husband by practicing on a therapist.

2. In a 1960 study, Schofied found that 90% of psychiatrists were predominantly males, in a 2 to one ratio, and that social workers were predominantly females in a ratio of 2 to 1.

3. A recent study by Boverman et al found that (1) there was high agreement among clinicians as to the attributes characterizing healthy adult men, healthy adult women and healthy adults, sex unspecified. (2) There was no difference among women & men clinicians. (3) Clinicians have different stan-

dards of health for men & women. These concepts of healthy mature women differ significantly from those for men & for adults. Clinicians are likely to suggest that women differ from healthy men by being more submissive, less independent, less adventurous, more easily influenced, less aggressive, less competitive, more excitable in minor crises, more easily hurt, more emotional, more conceted about their appearance, less objective and less interested in math & science.

From the above data (3) For a woman to be healthy she must "adjust" to and accept the behavioral norms for her sex even though these kinds of behavior are generally regarded as less socially desirable. The ethnic of mental health is masculine in our culture. Most clinicians, like most people in a patriarchal society have deep anti-female biases.

Since these anti-female biases, as stated in the Broverman study are equally common among women clinicians that men one cannot choose expect female clinicians to be automatically pro-female.

chaz chales Chesler suggests seems to make the suggestion that male mental

suggests\
Chesler advises that women patients should see women clinicians who are feminists.

Chesler also suggests that male psychologists, psychiatrists & social workers, as scientists, know nothing about women, and that they male clinicians should stop treating women altogether.

OR *IN*

Concepts of masculinity, femininity & adrogyny
Recent discontent with the standard rigid gender role stereotypes has brought about new concept called androgyny. Androgyny means having both masculine and feminine psychological characteristics. Androgynous people are free to adopt the most desirable characteristics of both gender-roles and incorporate them into their or culture or personality, or cultivate existing gens some gender and cross-gender traits. Additionally with an adrogynian concept the adoption and cultivation of traits can be done with a significantly reduced fear of being abnormal and maladjusted. Rigid adherence to a gender role can be stiffening: and adoption of androgyny can open horizons for additional growth. (It was considered that women adopting male behavior, or men adopting female behavior, were somehow sexually maladjusted. By the very nature of the androgynous concept there is not maladjustment.)

Some testing has been done to see if androgyny is really as good as it sounds. In a study, Androgynous & masculine people tend to be higher in self esteem than feminine undifferentiated people (Bem, 1977, Spence et al 1975) And in another study it has been found consistently that in ordering of groups, from highest to lowest in self esteem, androgyny is first followed by masculine, feminine & undifferentiated (Spence & Helmrich, 1978).

The concept of androgyny to is two dimensional allowing for a harmonious meshing of the 2 dimensions; the dimension of what we define as "masculine" and the dimension of what we call "feminine."

In the classroom this year Evelyn tried to take better notes. She doesn't think the writing itself helps her learn as much as "when I key myself in to listening, to taking notes. I have to pay attention in a certain way to write down something for later; so it's more how I have to key myself to listen."

When she has time, she writes her notes over; otherwise she just inspects them for correctness and suitability for review.

There's editing and lots of times, they [the notes] will go on "flash cards" which will usually stay home with me or in my purse, on index cards.— There's other editing, for example, I may have written something down at a time I didn't know whether it was important enough and later found out through further study it wasn't. That gets taken out. When I rewrite them [the notes], then they are more significant. I can understand much better. I can add something from the book or the class.

The concentration on writing was new to Evelyn.

The flash card idea came from the professor, and the idea was that a number of different kinds of learning are used: one, that you have to orally say the information when you read it off the flash card; and even writing out the flash cards was a way to practice recalling the information; putting it down on the card, you can see it visually. That was his [the professor's] idea, so I used it. And when I saw that it helped to write, I just did more, made notes, and so forth. . . .

Evelyn did not take "all this writing" on as "one awesome big thing"; in small steps she worked out a system of writing to learn. She writes in her personal life, as she puts it,

. . . yes, but only if I am in a great deal of difficulty, and I feel like I have to straighten things out in writing. I would write a note to myself or write out what I'm thinking about so that I could see it and see what's happening. . . . I use it for problem-solving, I use it (writing) for note-taking which is another kind of problem-solving.

Her other personal uses of writing include an occasional "real" letter, or a few unmailed ones. The latter serve "as a catharsis." When she does that, she knows she will not mail the letter; she just writes as a means of problem-solving.

If I'm really just messed up about something, and I haven't had anybody to talk to about it — because I'm more comfortable, so I try to write it out and look at it to see what's going on. And I read it; it's more like a letter to me. . . .

Writing assignments Evelyn finds most helpful in clarifying her thoughts include preparation for McGlynn's essay tests. McGlynn distributes five major study questions to her students prior to each examination. They prepare to answer all of them, a full spectrum of issues covered, and she selects one for the examination. While the preparation is difficult and time consuming, the essays are most useful in organizing newly gained information in an order that can make it more easily understood and retained.

For example:

1. There are three basic concepts of masculinity gender rules. These are: (1) a typology, (2) unidimensional or bipolar continuum, and (3) 2 dimensional or androgyny.

    The typology concept states that there are two kinds of people: "masculine ones" and "feminine ones." This represents the often accepted view that people must be one or the other gender, and it should match the persons biological sex. Requirements are that "feminine ones" act feminine & "masculine ones" act masculine. Criticisms of this area that it is very rigid and ignores variability from one woman to the next or one male to the next.

    The unidimensional, or bipolar continuum, concept is slightly more sophisticated stating that people can have varying degrees of "masculinity" or "femininity" on a continuum. Example:

Bipolar Continuum

very feminine (or male)	not very feminine (or male)

In this concept, people are allowed varying degrees of "normal" gender appropriate characteristics, however, no cross-gender adoption is included. This concept is also very restrictive and allows only a small degree of variability.

2. Discontent with rigid gender-role stereotypes have has brought about the "androgynous" concept. Androgyny means having both "male" & female" psychological characteristics. Androgynous people are free to adopt psychological characteristics of either the male or female gender-role or allows for cultivation of existing traits. Androgyny can mean, for those who find it desirable, freedom of personal expression without significant reduction in anxiety due to fear of non-conformity or fear of being somehow maladjusted.

Studies have been made to see if androgyny is as good as it sounds.

Androgynous and masculine people are higher in self-esteem than feminine and undifferentiated people. [(Bem 1977, Spence et all 1975) undifferentiated are are those who score low on both scales of the Bem Sex Role Inventory] Additionally, the ordering of groups, from high to low in self-esteem, is androgyny first, masculine, feminine and undifferentiated second, third & fourth respectively. (Spence & Helmreich 1978) In both studies, androgynous people are very high is self-esteem, an important psychological characteristic.

These results give find no evidence that androgynous people are maladjusted or suffering from confused gender-role identity.

The typology and bipolar continuum are both rigid in their assertion that masculinity and femininity are two *opposite* poles. The People are seen as either one, or degrees of either one, corresponding with biological sex. No cross-gender adoption is provided for in these 2 concepts. Behavior is very restricted.

The concept of androgyny does not view "masculinity" & "femininity"as opposite pole. but rather as

The concept of androgyny is 2 dimensional allowing for a comfortable meshing of the 2 dimensions: the masculine dimension and feminine dimension. Acceptable behavior is greatly expanded.

Diagrams

1. typology   femininity   masculinity

2. bipolar continuum

very feminine   not so feminine
(or very masculine)   (or not so
                                                      masculine)

3. two dimensional   very fem

                                      sphere of

not ————————————————— very masc.
very
masc.

Having readily admitted that she never thought about the role of writing in thinking or learning until recently, Evelyn goes on to say that, lately, she has been thinking about it . . .

. . . quite a bit, and I've spoken to somebody about it who said that writing was kind of a reflective process and . . ., I don't think I've done any deep thinking about it. . . . I've only noted that it does tend to work, most especially what intrigues me is my mathematics class where I probably do a great deal of writing, and it's very well programmed for me; I mean, I know exactly what to do, and I always have the information at hand, ready to recall and use on a test. All my test grades are good. And I do that kind of writing over and over and over again. I've been trying to figure out how I could transfer that kind of a process to another course because it works so well for me, in mathematics; to break it [material] down like that, but I haven't figured out how to do it yet. . . I think what I'm going to end up doing is, when I get the time, is to break down all of my subjects, the ones I like to take and probably will take the most, into some sort of logical pattern like the mathematics is broken up into and then write about them over and over. The interesting thing about the mathematics book is that the problems are given to you in the book as exercises to do, and they are very carefully thought out to bring in a single piece of information at a time. Whoever puts that together must think in a logical, mathematical manner, and I think it would be a wise idea to somehow use that same sort of problem solving in other courses . . . in that sort of step-by-step system.

Sometimes, Evelyn composes questions to help her learn.

Sometimes, I'm just really frustrated because I don't understand. The questions will go down on paper, so that I can find some kind of an outlet and then, maybe, try to find out later

on what's going on. Or it might hit me so deeply in a personal
sense that I'll write it down immediately.

She may not be able to ask a teacher for a long time, but she
will write down questions, then wait for a week to see which ones
really need to be answered. At that point, she can eliminate some
and ask the others.

> By process of elimination, some would drop off and others
> remain because, all week, I would just keep on writing ques-
> tions in lists, and as I thought about and reflected on them all
> week, some of them would fall into place. . . . Or maybe I
> would look the answer up.

Journal writing also proves comfortable and useful.

> . . . I wrote to myself — every day, every other day — for a
> period of a couple of months twice in the last two years. . . .
> I was really upset at the time, and there were so many things
> that I used to think about and reflect about that I didn't nec-
> essarily want to take to another person. I couldn't have re-
> cruited anybody to listen to me that long a period of time in
> the day, so I'd write something down and, maybe in a week,
> I would look it over and I could tell a lot from what was going
> on. When I'm unhappy and not really comfortable talking to
> people, I write it down. . . . Usually, when I listen to myself
> reading, the problem is already solved.

Evelyn puts her own learning theory into practice as she applies the systematically sequenced techniques found in her mathematics texts, with each successive problem adding only one new bit
of information, to comparable situations in other subjects. She
combines that strategy with her inclination to stay close to textual wording during the gradual mastery of a concept and depart-
ing from it en route to her own language, a process that parallels
increased understanding of the material. Here is an example from
her work on *hypothesis* and *variables* in "Educational Psychology."

Hypothesis
1. Hypothesis — a generalization that suggests a possible relationship between concepts but which has not yet been adequately confirmed by empirical evidence.
2. Hypothesis — a statement about an assumed relationship
   between two or more variables.
3. Hypothesis — a statement assuming a relationship between
   two or more variables.
4. Hypothesis — a statement proposing — or a statement of a
   proposed relationship between variables A and B.

Variables

(A) ——————— (B) (A and B are anything that is measureable), where the word "measureable" refers back to the statement concerning empirical evidence found in the original textual definition of "hypothesis."

The above reconstruction of the meaning of *hypothesis* and *variable* spans approximately two weeks and proceeds from the general to the specific. Toward the end, a marginal note focuses on recognition of and differentiation between dependent and independent variables.

In her sociology class, the concept of *ethnocentrism* undergoes the same treatment: a series of definitions which help her to bracket a clear working definition for herself.

1. the tendency to judge groups different from our own by the standards of our group.
2. imposing ideologies on other people
3. expanded group bias — *examples*
   a. the United States is the greatest country despite its faults
   b. Catholicism is the only true religion
   c. team A says: "We are better than team B."

Ultimately, she condenses these definitions and places them on a flashcard entitled "Forms of Ethnocentrism," on the reverse side of which appear the terms *nationalism, religious and ethnic bias*, and *racism*. This, for her, reinforces the knowledge which she has been constructing.

She makes similar notes on the term *variable*.

1. Variable — anything that is thought to have an influence on or be influenced by another thing.
   a. dependent — is the one that is being influenced
   b. independent — is the one doing the influencing
2. Variable — anything that, you believe, has an influence on something (A) or is influenced by something else (B).
   a. dependent — thing being influenced
   b. independent — thing that influences

Example: teacher "things" are influenced by student "things."

Evelyn then integrates this information into her detailed study of of the scientific method which includes, along with *hypothesis* and *variables*, exhaustive work on *quantification, measurement*, and *verification*, as well as *scientific attitude*, and including *objectivity, ethical neutrality, humility*, and *parsimony*. The latter Evelyn describes as "stinginess in that the scientific attitude accepts the simplest explanation." Her analysis of the scientific method and of some of its concepts leads again to flashcards synthesizing the work. The fact that the word *simplistic* is placed next to *parsimony* reflects her own point of view. Interestingly, the next flashcard in the series concerns *dogma*, which she defines as "a set of beliefs without any scientific basis."

Evelyn has developed a spectrum of ways to use writing for learning, beginning with simple recording of information for later use and/or reflective analysis. This process involves interpretation, redefinition, condensation, memorization, and application. The flashcards and the process leading up to their production are particularly helpful to her. The cards combine writing with oral repetition and with a visual stimulus. Thus, writing helps her incubate thought, record it, reformulate it, and, ultimately, encapsulate it for situational use.

Also, Evelyn shows unusual insight into the learning process. For example, she sees the value of sequencing writing assignments and other intellectual tasks in all content areas as it is done in mathematics, where only one unfamiliar bit of information is introduced at a time. As with some of the other students, she clearly perceives that writing can aid concentration, improve listening, enhance motivation, sharpen analysis and interpretation, aid memory, and generally provide a more fruitful climate for learning.

Kathy's Writing

Kathy looks and acts like a vivacious college coed rather than a young mother of teen-age children. She looks forward to classes with the enthusiasm of a high school graduate. Actually, entering college means a great deal to her. She has found key new ideas and expanded intellectual horizons. She is a busy housewife who has added a new dimension to her life, and she is eager to share her knowledge and excitement with her husband and children.

She has done considerable writing in each of her courses. She is convinced, for example, that once she writes down information, it sticks with her more than if she just reads it. "There's something about the connection with paper. It's more than just going over it." She also says,

> I write not just to remember, but to learn, to think about later. Any paper that I do, any test that I take, an essay or a report, I have to rewrite it constantly. . . . I think I use writing more than anything else to learn subject matter in the courses I'm taking now. Past courses involved reading over my notes; that's basically still writing. I was learning from my own writing,

whether it was notes from class or something I took out of a book. I lose it if I don't.

Her class notes, which trigger recall of things the teacher has said, are difficult for anyone else to read. They are cast in a personal, idiosyncratic shorthand used in the process of constructing knowledge from the information presented by teacher or text.

The "Psychology of Human Relations" writing has been like a mirror for myself, to bring out feelings and sort them into a certain pattern. That's been very helpful. If I just sit and think about it, it's not as helpful as when I write it down. It's better than looking in the mirror to me. When I go back and read this spontaneous writing, it shocks me. When you write it down off the top of your head, it's surprising what you come up with.

In the other psychology class, "Psychology of Women," all the tests are essays, and there are five subjects to investigate. Kathy has to write on all of them in preparation for the one the instructor will pick, but she has to know each one before she writes an essay on it.

I was worried about the essay tests because I'm not good at spontaneity. Learning comes harder to me than to other people. I have to really concentrate on it, and I found that if I wrote it down, just the fact of putting it down on paper, and then learning it is better than any other process I could follow. Certain things stick with me, but other, like facts, experiments and technical things, I have to write down.

Different kinds of assignments have proved useful in generating thought in the various subject areas. In nutrition, Kathy enjoyed doing the research for the required reports, as well as writing the reports, even though she found the subject "kind of dry." She has learned a great deal from rereading and rewriting, "picking things out" of different readings and research projects, and putting them in her own sequence. In "Psychology of Human Relations," she wrote to learn about herself and her surroundings, and she felt she has learned a great deal by doing so. In her writing for "Psychology of Women," she became quite emotional. She enjoyed the writing because she really wanted to do it. She has remembered more from that particular semester because of the writing.

. . . because I have to sit down and actually give myself enough time to write material, think about it, and absorb it; whereas last year, it was mostly class notes and going into short answer tests; I didn't retain as much.

Kathy has always enjoyed using writing for personal purposes. "It's a tremendous means of reflection. It's there, it's permanent." She found the practice of journal writing "a marvelous outlet, a tremendous enjoyment." To give herself 10 minutes or so just to write something out freely and then to go back and read what she had written: this was exciting and helpful.

She has pragmatically developed a number of writing-to-learn strategies. She uses "whatever works." She likes to learn, and writing seems to be a natural aid in doing so. Moreover, if something seems important and she wants to remember it, she writes it down. "If I don't, it gets lost in the shuffle." In fact, by her own account Kathy was spurred on to do more writing by her participation in this project. Now not only the teacher was reading her writing, but also other interested adults.

Class notes are important to Kathy, and she takes them carefully. She also makes careful marginal notes and uses both when she studies for tests. In addition, she writes questions in her books, and in her nutrition book she writes comments she may want her son or daughter to read later or that she may use to think about food shopping. Generally speaking, these notes and questions reflect "things that I want to change as a result of the course." In "Psychology of Women," I "raised a lot of questions in writing. Some I answered myself as I did more research on them; others I asked in class."

Kathy does other writing to prepare for class discussions or, in the case of nutrition, for oral presentations. First, she makes a rather comprehensive set of notes, and then she turns the notes into a final draft. In either case, she engages in multiple encounters with the material, and writing plays a central role: getting material out, organizing it, expanding upon it, or focusing on the main point.

She describes her composing process as follows:

> I have to more or less clear my head; find a quiet and comfortable place; make sure everything is there, and I don't have to get up again. I'll think about it for about an hour before I start to work to put myself in the mood for it, I guess. Then I'll sit down and start writing. A lot of things will come out, and then I have to make some kind of an outline form to contain the thoughts that come out; then I have to rearrange them.

Her sense of the audience for her writing greatly influences how she does it. In the "Psychology of Human Relations" journal, she writes for herself. Consequently, Kathy feels free to write without constraints. In the term paper for that course, she had to discuss a specific emotional learning problem. Because the paper was not for herself alone, she tried to eliminate emotional language and confine

herself to a more impersonal problem-solving approach. She reread
and rewrote the paper several times

> so that the paper was [oriented] for him, but the thoughts
> were still mine. For the first paper, I went back to the journal.
> It started to show me a real pattern of what I was doing. After
> two years of doing nothing, I was coming back to what I wanted
> to do: in other words, getting my life organized again. I took all
> that personal material and made it more factual, more objective.
> It was almost like feedback, as if I had been sitting there talking
> to a psychiatrist and all of a sudden, I felt as if he had recorded
> myself and then listened to it. When you're saying or writing
> something, it's feeling, but when you read it, it's there in black-
> and-white. It's proof that you're the one that said it.

Kathy tries to allow herself enough time to rough draft her
work, staying with it until she gets tired or until she begins "dragging
with thoughts." Then, she leaves the writing and comes back to it
later, when she is fresh, and begins rearranging it. The third time she
returns to the writing, she does some further rearranging and rewriting. Each time, the writing becomes a bit more organized, more "like
the finished product."

The first draft of her paper on women in therapy, using Naomi
Weisstein's article, shows considerable emotional and intellectual
turmoil.

[First Draft]

> Ms. Weisstein very adeptly points out how our present day psy-
> chology on women is truly useless and bound to the past by a
> lack of research on what women are really like or what women
> want or need much less what makes a women function in our
> modern society. I use the word "modern" loosely because I'm
> not sure "we have come a long way, baby." Our machinery and
> appliances are up to date and well advanced, but the basic fact
> remains women are still *behind* those appliances & machinery.
> A small number of women have advanced to higher positions
> but the sad truth remains, society as a whole expects a woman
> to be nurturing, mother & wife and have a career as a secondary
> goal, if at all.
>
> Ms. Weisstein's view of psychology & how is not limited to
> women only, rather (how people act & who they are) it has
> failed to understand the reasons people act as they do & what
> might change their actions.
>
> Ms. Weisstein's view of psych (how people act & who they
> are) is not limited to women only, rather its failure to under-

stand the reasons people act as they do what might change their actions.

Evidence has been accumulating — that what people do and who they believe they are is in general a function of what people around them expect them to do or be or what their surroundings imply they should be or do . . . footnote pg. 223.

Ms. Weisstein points out the basis for most therapy is based on theories of Freud, Erikson, and others experimenter bias, theories without evidence, experiments used to support the hypothesis of the experimenter such as primate behavior, reports of differences and non-reports on similarities.

In 1952, H. J. Ensench reported a study of "victim therapy" wherein 44% improvement rate among patients in psychoanalysis, 64% rate psychotherapy and 72% improvement among patients receiving no treatment.

"Research studies in psychotherapy tend to be concerned more with psychotherapeutic *procedure* and less with outcome . . . to some extent it reflects an interst in the psych. situation as a kind of personality lab." J. B. Rotter

I tend to agree with Ms. Weisstein's overall view of psychology and its definite lack of true research on women. However, since it's presently the "main event" in therapy I feel we must work with it in an effort to improve its usage and bring about a new awareness of what women want and what makes women act or react as they do. Until we, ourselves as women are capable of seeing or feeling equal to men we will never be able to change our surroundings which is exactly what seems to shape our present status as women. Unless we break the chain of events our future women will be writing similar articles 50 years or more from now. It's been a long hard to reach as far as we have, we have only just begun to raise our consciousness to a level of being aware of the deficiency in the systems, but awareness is the only way to start making such progress. (change this ending)

Kathy began this draft by drawing a series of inferences from the premise contained in the statement "we have come a long way, baby." This statement represented a point of insight for her, and she has used it fully. At the same time, she has gone back over this handwritten draft to fill it with personal digressions and arrows to be used for later reorganization. The marginal note that she made at the end ("change this ending") signals the need she feels to move toward a less emotional, more intellectual tone. The second draft and the third and final draft, which follow, reflect this movement.

[Second Draft]

Pg 207   End like
                until we ourselves as women are
                capable of seeing ourselves as equals
                to men we will never rid society of
     Women is made not born   the backslide as to what women
     construct the female   Psych of really are

Ms. Weisstein very adeptly points out how useless our present
psychology is on women truly is is truly useless and bound to
the past by a lack of research on what makes a woman function
in our modern society. I use the word "modern" loosely because
I'm not really sure "we have come a long way, baby." Our surroundings are modern & up to date, our appliances & machinery
are well advanced but the basic fact is we as women are still
behind those appliances & machines. What is even sadder is the
fact that society as a whole (man women included) feels that
is where we belong, even if we take on a career "equal" to a
man, we are still expected to keep our place as a nurturing,
mother, wife role! The basics of all most study research still
reverts back to Freud and his "years of intensive clinical research" none of which has been tested & confirmed, but passed
on from one psyc. to another — try pg. 210 research as the
xxxxxxxxxx

The first typed copy (the third draft) is considerably more
focused and adds a metaphor at the end to destroy the stereotype
of the ingredients of femininity as "sugar and spice." And significantly, in the last paragraph Kathy asks, "Where do we start to make
changes?" This question, if she is to begin answering it in this paper,
thus exerts a planning function. It forces her to look beyond the
position she has developed to this point and to examine possible
courses of action.

[Third Draft]

Ms. Weisstein, in her article "Psychology constructs the female"
very adeptly points out how our present psychology of women
is truly useless and bound to the past by a lack of research on
what women want or need, much less what makes a women
function in our modern society. I use the word modern loosely
because I'm not sure "we have come a long way, baby."
    Ms. Weisstein's view of psychology and its failure to under-
stand the reasons people act as they do and what might change

their actions is not limited to women, but includes men. Personality psychologists have been accumulating evidence that what people do and who they believe they are is, in general, a function of what people around them expect them to do or be, or what their surroundings imply they should be or do. Ms. Weisstein points out that most therapy is based on theories of Freud, Erikson, on experimenter bias, theories without evidence, experiments used to support experimenter hypothesis, such as primate behavior, reports of differences and non-reports of similarity.

In 1952 Eysenck reported on a study of "outcome of therapy" wherein there was a 44% improvement among patients in psychoanalysis, 64% improvement of those in psychotherapy and 72% improvement among patients receiving no treatment. J. B. Rotter states "research studies in psychotherapy tend to be concerned more with psychotherapeutic procedure and less with outcome . . . to some extent it reflects an interest in the psychotherapy situation as a kind of personality lab."

I agree with Ms. Weisstein's overall view of psychology and the definite lack of true research of women. However, I feel we must work with therapy limits in an effort to improve it, and bring about a new awareness of what women want and what makes women act or react as they do.

Until women are capable of feeling an equality in society, there will never be any real change in social expectations, which is precisely what appears to shape our present status as second class majority. Unless we break the negative chain of events (social expectation/self-fulfilling prophecy/confirmation of social expectations) our future women will be writing similar articles 50 years from now.

Where do we start to make changes? Since knowledge is power, we must work to bring about an awareness of what women are made of, and it isn't always "sugar and spice."

Notes:

H. J. Eysenck, "The Effects of Psychotherapy: An Evaluation." *Journal of Consulting Psychology* 16 (1952), 319–324.

J. B. Rotter, "Psychotherapy." *Annual Review of Psychology* 11 (1960), 381–414.

Kathy's analysis of Phyllis Chesler's article, while more subdued in tone, still expresses her difficulty in suppressing anger and dealing with such emotionally charged issues in a detached manner. The initial draft clarifies the issues, and the final draft shows the results of her reworking of both the ideas and the language.

[Initial Draft]

After reading Phyllis Chesler's article "patient and Patriarch"
I know we have *not* "come a long way baby!" I realize just
how far my head has been stuck in the sand for so long a time.
I shutter to think how many other women are next to me in
the same sand box. When I first started reading Ms. Chesler's
statistics I thought perhaps the high percentage of women
in therapy could possibly relate to the openness women are
capable of in discussing problems. It would appear this is not
the case at all, but again a show of male dominance through
male orientedₗpsychology in a stereotyped role of submissive
　　　　　　└ society? society? (＿＿＿) feel
"Patient" and "Patriarch" doctor. We are so brain washed so
to think the female therapist (with male made oriented trim-
ming) is somehow less qualified than lesser than the male
therapist —
Is there no end to the subliminal oppression of most of us
　　　　　　She ⌐　　⌐themselves
　Ms. Chester's shows therapist actually prefer to treat female
patients over male patients (this brings up the question of the
disservice therapists are doing not only to women but to men.
Do therapists subconsciously encourage women to go into therapy for their own (therapeutic) qualifications? Do male therapists tend to overlook similar symptoms in men to shore up
their own egos?)

　Once again male has given us an explanation for our frustra-
tions of oppression in his therapy which feeds his ego and pock-
etbook not to mention keeping us in line.

　Male gives us reasons for why we feel like we do which keeps
us in line with male theories never knowing what women are
really about

　It appears to me women are molded from the moment of
birth more by men than any other so far considered factor,
such as anatomy or even environment. Male oriented beliefs
& ideas even form the basis of the mother that gives birth to
the female child.

　As Ms. Chesler asks in her article, where do women begin to
change make changes. I believe women must first develop a
bond among themselves. Women have forever been divided &
conquered by males. I think Ms. Chesler's suggestion of anyone
in therapy to seek guidance from women therapists who are
feminists is an excellent *beginning*. It seems to me things of the
hasn't even been touched yet. Women in general know that

something is wrong, but missing but few know exactly what it is, much less where to stand making changes.

I think the beginning comes with awareness which one of consciousness.

It occurs to me that the majority of women are not even conscious of just how male oriented — dominated our lives are.

But what about the thousands of women who are not in therapy for lack of money or other reasons?

[Final Draft]

After reading Phyllis Chesler's article "Patient & Patriarch" I know we have not "come a long way, baby!" I realize just how far my head had been stuck in the sand for so long a time. I shudder to think how many other women are in the same sand box.

When I first started reading Ms. Chesler's study I thought perhaps the high percentage of women in therapy could possibly relate to the way most women are capable of disguising problems. It would appear this is not the case at all, but again a show of male dominance through male oriented psychology in a stereotyped role of submissive patient and doctor Patriarch. A role in which the therapist allows women to find the reasons for feeling as they do and then "adjust" to the role of being a woman as defined by a man. The role man has created for women.

Ms. Chesler's comparison between therapy and marriage as the two accepted mediums for women is excellent, one I had never considered but agree with totally. Any divergence from our prescribed role is socially labeled maladjusted.

Ms. Chesler also points out society (both male & female) feels the female therapist (with the same male oriented training) is somehow less qualified than the male therapist. Further study shows therapists themselves actually prefer to treat female patients over male patients.

It appears to me, women are, from the moment of birth molded more by men than any other so far considered factor, such as anatomy or even environment. Male oriented beliefs & ideas even form the basis of the mother that gives birth to the female child.

As Ms. Chesler asks in her article, where do women begin to make changes? I believe, we women must first develop a bond among ourselves. Women have forever been divided and conquered by man. I think Ms. Chesler's suggestion to any who are in therapy to seek guidance from women therapists who are feminists is an excellent beginning.

But what about the thousands of women who are not in therapy for one reason or another? It occurs to me that the majority? of women are not conscious of just how male oriented & dominated our lives really are.

Perhaps one "small step" for women would begin with the change of our the female image as seen by society through the media, advertising and the like.

Kathy's treatment of "women in the media," which follows, is softer in tone. Much of her anger, it would seem, has been spent on the issues raised for her by Phyllis Chesler's article. Consequently, she can handle the issues and the writing of this next paper with greater equanimity. In this case, the final draft differs little from the first draft. Kathy makes a few corrections and that's all.

[Initial Draft]

Advertising on television and in magazines is the mirror "image" of how society sees the women. Advertising doesn't create the beautiful, not too bright, floor cleaning "lady of the house" but it does perpetuate the image. Doesn't everyone become ecstatic over the smell of freshly laundered towels & underclothes? Isn't every women (under 41 that is) thankful for the turtles giving up their precious oils to keep us younger looking?

I was delighted to find Lucy Komisan's artiels

I was surprised to discover in Lucy Komisan's article that there are advertising agencies that are attempting to make changes in the stereotyped roles of women.

I think *TV has an enormous impact on a large amount of people.* I can't help often wonder what the response would be if the advertising agencies exposed the viewers to a different image of woman. Instead of the women executive behind the big desk who losing a big deal because she's worried about a run in her stocking, why not just show the logical reasons for buying the stockings, such as to give the legs a hint of color, etc.

I have seen a few attempts to show women in a better light but we have far to go. One good thing about the "not too bright" image that women see every day in advertising is that there is a new awareness of how we are seen by society. All of us must become angry enough to do something to make the changes in our image.

In her journal and in these papers, writing helps Kathy to focus on those pieces of information or those opinions or those conclusions that she finds personally telling. She uses the writing, especially the movement from first draft to final product, to understand why women are still "behind the appliances" and to pose the question of how women might begin making the changes that she feels are necessary. We see Kathy working out her point of view in relation to the readings and discussions in the course. Thus, she is not just summarizing the main points of an article to show the teacher she can do it, or repeating facts to demonstrate that she has them at hand, but she is genuinely working on the alteration of her own consciousness, and the writing is a powerful tool in this process. Whether the final products are "good" pieces of writing is not the main issue, for this is not a writing course. It is a course on the psychology of women, and the issue is for all the students to confront information and issues in ways that transform their thinking and their consciousness.

Like other students described in this volume, Kathy writes to recall things as well as to think and learn. She is perhaps as acutely aware as any that we can learn from and through our writing. The fact that she is unusually comfortable with writing essay tests is due to the multiple-draft approach and the advance preparation encouraged in McGlynn's class. In this course and in "Psychology of Human Relations," Kathy learned a great deal about herself through freewriting and journal writing. She also discovered, in Odell's (1980) words, that "writing gives thoughts permanence."

Other students in McGlynn's course confirmed Kathy's experience of writing to learn. As they said, whether one writes out answers to questions contained in course objectives or uses writing to work out ideas while reading, the results include better problem solving and greater learning by induction. By consensus, this group also confirmed the value of careful rewriting of notes, agreeing that writing "stamps information into the brain," that it builds confidence and reinforces the special vocabulary of each discipline, and that writing to think is the opposite of, and the antidote to, the practice of rote regurgitation of information.

Writing in Mathematics

Donald Reichman is a contemplative young mathematician with a gentle manner and a subtle sense of humor. While working with a group of incorrigible youthful offenders at a juvenile detention facility, a group who were less than eager to learn science and mathematics, he induced them to unburden themselves in writing. Reichman's interest in the power of writing to unlock the mind dates from that experience. These 120 "seriously damaged" kids had done horrible things, had been sent to reform schools, and then had been sent to this first rung on the ladder of prisons. He remarked,

> . . . the last six months before my departure, I decided the last thing they needed to learn was science and math at that point in their lives. I closed the door and started having them do writing about what was going on in their heads. There was incredible hostility, anger. These kids were writing pages and pages about frustration, about how they were feeling. It would seem to me it was much more exciting than any mathematics or science they could have been doing. I was reading to them, and they were writing reactions to what I read to them about prisons and crime, so I really got off on what writing could do from that experience. After that I made the connection that writing could do other things beside tell stories.

Since that time, Reichman has periodically experimented with writing to explore the ways in which it can be used for thinking, problem-solving, and learning in mathematics.

For this experiment, Reichman assigned mathematical problems in "Basic Mathematics" and in "Calculus" that were just a bit too difficult for his students to complete. The instructions were identical. They were asked to try to solve the problems numerically. However, if they reached an impasse, they were to write of their difficulties, using writing as a means to find alternate strategies that might help them solve the problems.

When Reichman asks his students to solve problems through writing, he expects them to use writing to understand a problem they were unable to understand before. In his view, an effective writing assignment enables students to write about the relationship between problems they can and can't do. If they can say: "I solved another problem this way, but in this problem it's not the same. Here's what seems to be different about it." Eventually, if they can make a connection by isolating the source of the impasse, they have made a quantum leap.

Upon completion of the experiment, he gave us several papers from each group. He also put us in touch with some students who were willing to talk about their experience and views. But, most importantly, he spent some time sharing his views on both groups of learners and their degree of success in using writing as an aid to numerical problem-solving.

At the same time, Reichman was talking to English teachers about thinking, asking their views on what thinking was all about. We are all, he believed, involved in doing and teaching thinking. As a consequence, each of us should use other disciplines in teaching our own. For example, he is convinced that if English teachers were more comfortable with mathematics they might be able to use the deductive skills that go into solving a mathematical problem as another way of teaching argument and paragraphing in composition.

In this instructor's view, basic math students have encountered mostly failure, are afraid to take risks, and tend to elect to write only if they are confident they can do the problem anyway. They feel good about having solved the problem and write what they are doing, more as a process description than as an instrument of thought.

The instruction was — I showed them how to find the lowest common denominator with this method, which is hard — and several students were not able to pick up what I was doing, so I said, "That's fine, you're not able to understand what I'm doing here. I'd like you to write what it is you are doing, and maybe that will open the door to how it should be done. In other words, maybe the writing will force you to think about what's going on here, and your new thoughts will allow you to do what is to be done." Here's one person who understood the assignment and here's another. They both wrote about it, but mostly about how they didn't understand. Those who understood it all wrote step-by-step, like a recipe, but it worked for them.

Learning, in Reichman's view occurs when there is "some kind of acquisition of knowledge that maintains itself for a certain period of time." Learning implies the ability to perform certain tasks through memorized or understood skills. Memorized skills can serve as a point of departure for other skills. The more intuition is necessary, as in algebra, the more understanding, and therefore learning, is possible. According to Reichman, learning is "one giant continuum," and we are all somewhere on it. In mathematics especially, learning cannot be defined as being different for basic and advanced learners.

You could say that learning is not learning unless it can be applied, but it doesn't have to be. What is knowledge? Perhaps that could be the ultimate test of it. In mathematics, it is not easy to apply it. Even outstanding students may have difficulty in seeing that.

He characterizes mathematics, particularly algebra, as a universal language. Advanced algebra uses the same language as elementary algebra, arithmetic, or calculus. We just keep building on it, increasing our vocabulary, as it were.

In his personal life, Reichman writes letters occasionally. Sometimes, when he has things he wants to work out, he makes charts. Usually he favors a dual symbol system. For philosophical problems, he may also draw pictures.

> It seems fairly clear that what writing does is force you to think. The problem with mathematics is that sometimes it's not clear what to think about. I find that when I ask students what they're thinking about when they are stuck on a problem, they're not thinking about anything in particular. So I feel as if writing would at least force them to stay involved with the problem. It's kind of like a baseball player who gets up to bat convinced he can't hit the ball: won't even look at it and just sort of stands there looking into right field or left field, wherever, not looking at the ball. Writing in mathematics may not make them swing, but [it] still keeps them looking at the ball. That sounds like a better idea than looking out into the bleachers.

This interesting metaphor underlies his belief that using writing in mathematics to work out of an impasse must be especially helpful for students who are fairly secure about themselves and will freewrite to let themselves and their instructor see their reasoning process. In just this way, Reichman uses writing to find out what he was (or is) thinking, especially at times when he wrestles with intense academic or philosophical problems. To study students' mathematics anxiety, Reichman has them keep math journals because, in his view, writing helps us to explore feelings as well as thoughts. He remarked that

> as far as mathematics or writing anxiety is concerned that is really what it's about, understanding how you feel about this subject and trying to get over it. It ties in with, maybe if you know more about it, then maybe you can get over it. So I think journal writing is important as far as that goes. You can say, "Yesterday I was feeling this way when I was doing this problem, and it's the same way I feel when I see X whom I hate."

He is convinced that writing has this problem-solving potential, helping to clarify and organize thinking. In studying computers again, he finds the process somewhat like writing. A task someone doesn't think he or she is capable of doing suddenly comes within reach: "The computer likes sentences. You write a sentence, then another, and somehow, you're able to make this computer do what you didn't think you could do." He remembers writing papers in which he was suddenly able to prove a point that he didn't think he could prove or where the amount of material was so large that it seemed impossible to organize. Yet, through writing and the thinking it helps generate, you work on the material

> and suddenly, there it is! You've made the connection. Or in a mathematical problem where you don't think you're going to be able to prove this thing, but through a series of steps, there it is, and you are able to prove it.

Reichman walks around the classroom, looking at what students are doing and giving them immediate feedback. The feedback is intended to guide them, not necessarily to put them on the right track, but to push them off the wrong one and then to hope that they can take it from there. Only if all such indirect means of assistance fail does he say what the right track is, telling them then, "Now you finish it." In grading exams, he circles wrong answers and gives pointers as to how the correct answers should be found. He tells students before he returns the papers,

> these are the kinds of comments you can expect. If I don't follow what's going on, I'll say "huh?" or just put a question mark which implies that there's some kind of faulty reasoning going on there. There's got to be humor in the whole thing.

In the course of submitting the problem-solving papers from Reichman's calculus class, two students of widely different backgrounds and circumstances discussed their perception of the experiment, as well as their view of writing to learn in other areas. Graham, an articulate college graduate with a degree in economics who was taking an evening calculus course which he needed for his present position, and Frank, a young surveyor's apprentice taking it for upward mobility, found themselves collaborating on an educational issue rather than looking at each other across a social and philosophical gulf. In their conversation, they responded to the same questions in turn and also "bounced ideas off each other."

Graham always found that rewriting his lecture notes and paraphrasing textbook passages in his own words helped him learn more because these activities aided him in formulating and clarifying his own ideas. They fostered active thought about the material. Frank's mechanics course involved problems in trigonometry, over and over, but there were different formulas and different ways of writing them. If he couldn't approach a certain problem one way, he then wrote about it, putting in new variables and coming up with the answer.

"You could see an example in the book and that's not going to do nothing," Frank said. "Were you verbalizing it or just writing it over and over?" Graham asked.

"It was a mathematical statement in words but in my own mind, I was talking it over and trying to understand the problem. . . ." was Frank's reply.

Since Frank has taken no humanities courses in college, he felt unqualified to comment on writing to learn in the humanities, but he pointed out that the material that sticks with him in a subject like biology is that which he has researched and written papers about. Suddenly he exclaimed, "This has nothing to do with school, but as far as expressing myself, I express myself sometimes better by writing than by speaking. Say, if me and my girlfriend have an argument, and you could argue back and forth for, say, hours, and just rehash everything. You condense everything in a letter, the way you seriously feel, without the pressure of direct . . ."

"Confrontation?" Graham interjected.

"Yes, like that you can really accomplish something and put your thoughts down, I think . . ."

In turn, Graham indicated that he has used writing for learning in diverse areas. In econometrics, he wrote analyses of material to come up with the meaning underlying his mathematical statements. In macroeconomics also, talking about and writing down ideas helped him considerably in understanding topics which were not inherently verbal in their presentation. Frank then remarked, "that comes into play in what we are doing right now in calculus in the applications of say, the integrals. Like you may be able to do integration, the mathematics, but then when it comes down to mathematical problems, and applying it, when you have to read through mathematical problems, it's a whole different ball game."

Graham agreed, saying "You're right. If you understand the connotation of the applications of the mathematics you're studying, you'll be able to do better at applying it to your environment, and writing is certainly helpful there."

Frank agreed, adding that when Reichman first asked them to reason out a relatively difficult problem in writing, he didn't think he could put his ideas into words to help solve the problem he was working on.

Reichman said, "Just put down thoughts as they come to you. Don't worry about their context or nothing. Just make them make sense."

Frank said, "So I was just putting down thoughts as they were coming to me, and by the time I was done, they weren't as jumbled as I thought they were. They kind of made sense in the long run."

Graham observed, "I did the same things, and I found that it helped me a great deal. When I first started the problem, I couldn't figure out the best way to do it, but as I kept writing, in terms of 'what if I try this approach? or another?' I solved the problem, so I was quite surprised."

Frank continued, "When I was first asked to do it, I really didn't think that it would help or . . . make any sense, but it did turn out that it was a real helpful tool. At the end of my paragraph, I had almost answered my own questions about what I was doing wrong."

[Calculus — Frank]

Looking at #6, I can see the $u = 2x - 1$ and $du = 2dx$. When I looked at this problem,

$$\frac{X^2 + 1}{x}$$

I figured I could solve this the same way. I solved $x(x^2 - x)dx$ by just multiplying it out or in this case by x, but I used the wrong type of division. I should have done simple division instead of using the quotient rule.

In this "natural experiment" in calculus, Frank used writing to find the solution to problem six. He began erroneously, applying the same method as in problem five. However, he soon found that, while the technique was appropriate for five, it was inadequate for solving six. He recognized his error through writing, and subsequently he came upon the right solution.

Graham sits down and tries to finish as much as he can at one sitting. Otherwise, he loses ideas that were beginning to formulate but, because they were never written, remain unrealized. If his writing is interrupted, and thus divided into several sittings, Graham may end up throwing away much of his material.

Frank, on the other hand, doesn't want to stop if he was "hot on an idea," really producing. With short papers, Frank agrees with Graham about first writing out all the ideas, letting them run wild, going back, reading them over, seeing what needs weeding out, then polishing them for submission. In surprise, Graham asks, "You don't do that on every paper?" and Frank responds by saying that sometimes he prefers to free-write a portion, say a paragraph, then polish it before going on to the next portion.

In writing to problem-solve in the calculus experiment, Graham posed the problem in the form of a question addressed to himself.

[Calculus — Graham]

$$\int_{}^{4} \frac{X^2 + 1}{x} \, dx \qquad\qquad u = X^2 + 1$$
$$du = 2x$$

How do I make $\dfrac{X^2 + 1}{x}$ into a u from which I can create a du?

Can I divide x into $X^2 + 1$? Does it equal $x + 1$? If so . . .

$$\int_{1}^{4} X + 1 \, dx \qquad\qquad u = x + 1$$
$$du = 1 \, dx$$

Is this correct?

Carrying through, assume it is

$$\int_{1}^{4} X + 1 \, dx, \ \frac{X^2}{2} \, dx, \ \frac{1}{2}x^2 \qquad\qquad 8 - \frac{1}{2} = \frac{71}{2} = \frac{15}{2}$$

Assuming $\dfrac{X^2 + 1}{x}$ does not equal $X + 1$ that $X^2 + 1$ divided by x does equal $x + 1$.

Another approach $X^{-1/2} (X^2 + 1) = X^{3/2} + X^{-1/2}$

$$\int_{1}^{4} X^{3/2} + X^{-1/2} \, dx = \qquad u = x \qquad u = x$$
$$du = x \qquad du = x$$

$$\frac{2}{5} \times \frac{5}{2} = 2 \times \frac{1}{2} \quad \begin{smallmatrix}4\\1\end{smallmatrix} \qquad\qquad \frac{84}{5} - \frac{12}{5} = \frac{72}{5}$$

Graham did express concern about whether this kind of trial-and-error approach might result in lower test grades. However, both students agreed that a teacher who valued writing for learning would not object to a revelation of their thinking processes, even on a test. On the contrary, the instructor would likely be pleased if a student became more relaxed and more successful with a problem that seemed unfigurable at first glance. By the end of the paragraph of writing, they both think, a problem may well be broken down and on its way to solution. Frank also felt that this kind of problem-solving process, which includes writing, benefits the mathematics student by slowing him or her down and preventing careless errors.

Nevertheless, both planned a strategy for justifying the use of writing to reason their way back on to the right track in a testing situation with a sceptical teacher. Graham began,

If I followed wrong paths to get to the right path and along the way, I came upon some totally illogical statements, if it took me a while to figure out that they were wrong, and I finally found the right path, I guess, I could scratch the top part.

Frank added,

plus, as you were going along, and you had written your paragraph, and you had gone like from one direction to another and finally found where you had made your mistake, then you could kind of censor it and write it mathematically toward your solution. . . .

No one really ever suggested it to Graham, but he "kind of" thought that if he wrote something down, he would learn it better. When he writes things down, he doesn't copy verbatim. He rearranges words and ideas in a format that seems logical to him. He "guesses" that is what using writing to think and learn is all about.

In discussing the carry-over of writing to learn to their jobs, the two students differed. Frank didn't think that it would be applicable in his surveying work because it would be too time consuming. To Graham, writing is extremely important in communicating with people.

. . . in office memos, you condense your ideas down to a logical format. You're stating exactly what you mean, instead of just playing around with words: or for writing ideas for what your firm can do, where we should be going, or just ideas on what went wrong with something, or suggestions you think an employee should follow up on. Written communication, especially in our present technological society, is becoming more and more important.

The inquiry now shifted toward the differences between writing for oneself and writing for someone else. Frank suggested that we try to write more coherently for someone else. A brief, even cryptic, note to ourself often suffices because the rest of the message is in our head anyway. Graham added that "if one were going to give a speech, writing beforehand about what he is going to say, so that he has a logical, concrete format instead of rambling would be a rather good idea."

When asked what kinds of assignments they have found most helpful in promoting thinking and learning, Frank favored something that would make a person dig for information and gain more knowledge in the process. He also feels comfortable in writing for personal purposes, while Graham prefers writing to inform or motivate others.

The closest he has come to journal writing is his seasonal sales book in which he logs sales results, best sellers, customer preferences, and factors affecting sales such as weather or recessionary influences. However, when he was in high school, he kept a "semi" poetry book. He wrote "a whole bunch of poems" about questions concerning his existence. It was "problem-solving on a macrolevel" (as opposed to "personal problem solving"). While Frank has never kept anything like a journal, he frequently writes series of questions, finding a relationship among them and compiling them into a broader question that would elicit one answer to all of them from someone else.

When asked whether they ever used written questions to promote thinking, Frank said, "Not usually," but Graham said,

> A little while ago, I wrote a program of exercises that I would do regularly, and maybe the question I had before I wrote the booklet is "How come I'm not doing these exercises?" and I came up with the idea of writing them all down and did sort of a journal to keep track of everything like that. . . . Maybe indirectly, you sort of ask yourself questions, do things like that to answer them. Sometimes you have to know what you want to know in order to go after it.

Graham also writes questions in terms of objectives: "How can I achieve this? How can I go back to school? How can I get a better job?" Sometimes he writes down the answers, depending upon the importance he attributes to them. He also likes keeping lists of what he needs to do, in order of importance. He also prepares for a speech or debate by writing an outline or notes on index cards of the subject to be discussed. Frank feels strongly about the usefulness of writing in the middle of a discussion to capture a good thought or idea because "by the time it's done, you may not be thinking of it."

At the beginning of short assignments, Graham's writing process consists of "pretty much just rambling." He first "accesses" all his information, trying to get it down in some kind of order and to create an outline of exactly what he wants to write and what results he is trying to get from it. Once he has finished a draft, he redoes it until he has a satisfactory end result. On longer assignments, his process is similar except that he does less rewriting because he has less time.

When rewriting, Graham first tries to get a flow of ideas and statements that make sense and will stimulate someone to read the work. Above all, from the very beginning, he is interested in the logical context: "Where am I trying to go?" Graham tackles structure last: "It is something that has to be done," he says.

The student volunteers in "Basic Mathematics" didn't want to be interviewed or identified. Thus, they became known as Student A and Student B. And, as Reichman discovered, "Basic Math" students tend to be insecure and thus are reluctant to use writing during the problem-solving process. Either they simply don't know how, or they don't wish to have their thought processes, about which they are very uncomfortable, exposed for the teacher to see. So, instead of using writing *in* the process, they use it as a means of reflection on their thought processes after they have completed work on a problem. In this way, the writing serves more as a means of documenting and verifying their method or solution.

Student A was inventive in her choice of a problem which was of practical value and, thereby, less intimidating than other available problems. She volunteered to increase a recipe for six to serve 14 people. Student B, on the other hand, combined writing with a statement of the problem and a list of the original ingredients, then dealt with the solution in proportions expressed in fractions. Nonetheless, it did seem to have been a useful exercise for them.

[Student A]

Short Ribs of Beef with Peaches
Serves 6 people
I will increase this recipe to serve 14 people

(1) 2T cooking oil
(2) 3 lbs of beef short ribs
(3) 2 cups of water
(4) 1 pkg of onion soup mix
(5) 2t powdered ginger
(6) 29 oz sliced peaches (canned)
(7) 2T soy sauce
(8) 3T cornstarch
(9) 1 green pepper chopped

Heat oil in a dutch oven skillet, brown short ribs on all sides, add water, onion soup mix, and ginger; simmer for two hours in covered dutch oven. Combine juice from peaches, corn starch, soy sauce and chopped pepper in a bowl. Add to beef mixture, bring to boil, lower heat and stir until sauce thickens. Add peaches & serve.

In mathematical terms:

(1) $\dfrac{2T}{6} = \dfrac{?}{14}$? = 4.6T

(2) $\dfrac{3\text{ lbs}}{6} = \dfrac{?}{14}$? = 7 lbs

(3) $\dfrac{2C}{6} = \dfrac{?}{14}$? = 4.6C

(4) $\dfrac{1\text{ pkg}}{6} = \dfrac{?}{14}$? = 2.3 pkgs

(5) $\dfrac{2t}{6} = \dfrac{?}{14}$? = 4.6t

(6) $\dfrac{29\text{ oz}}{6} = \dfrac{?}{14}$? = 67.6 oz

(7) $\dfrac{2T}{6} = \dfrac{?}{14}$? = 4.6T

(8) $\dfrac{3T}{6} = \dfrac{?}{14}$? = 7T

(9) $\dfrac{1\text{ gp}}{6} = \dfrac{?}{14}$? = 2.3 gp

Student B was even less adventurous than Student A. He chose a straightforward equation as his "natural experiment" problem. Throughout he displayed a thorough understanding of the process and arrived at a clear solution.

[Student B]

Numerical Problem:

(4 − 3)[2 − 3(2 − 1)]

Verbalization:

The quantity four minus three (4 − 3) is multiplied by the problem inside the brackets. The quantity of 2 minus one, which is inside the brackets, is multiplied by 3, which is outside of its parentheses. This answer is added to "2," which is the quantity (4 − 3) and the answer from inside the brackets.

The function of Student B's written commentary was to clarify for himself and others what he instinctively knew was correct. Rather than using writing as a blueprint or as a means of trouble-shooting, Student B used writing to describe a process and to verify its success, thus providing an ego boost and a means of reflection at the same time.

The "natural experiment" in mathematics underscored the idea that writing can serve as a valuable aid in numerical problem-solving, particularly in areas where alternate solutions to problems are desirable. The students from "Calculus" and "Basic Mathematics" represent the opposite ends of the spectrum of mathematics achievement and attitude. Consequently, they approached and used writing in quite different ways. Frank and Graham, for example, became so involved in issues concerning writing, thinking, and learning that they virtually conducted the interview by themselves. Their interaction was exciting to observe. Frank advocated using writing for making connections between theoretical and applied knowledge in mathematical as well as more personal problem-solving and for capturing ideas to keep them from "fleeing." Graham emphasized the importance of individual construction of knowledge in the learner's own language. He favored using writing for a variety of purposes outside of academia: memos, planning, and speech preparation are among them. Both he and Frank considered writing the best tool for analysis. Their cases also demonstrate how an instructor can support their growth in mathematics through the use of writing for thinking and learning.

In "Calculus," the approach was more abstract and theoretical, and so were the students' thought processes. They represented a genuine search for alternative solutions. In "Basic Mathematics," the purpose of writing turned out to be more for reinforcement of procedure and of the accuracy of the achieved solution. In both cases, writing did help the students stay focused on the problem, an important contribution in itself. If cultivated on a regular basis as a central part of mathematics work, writing could become a valuable concomitant of mathematical thinking, problem-solving, and learning.

5

Writing, Teaching, and Learning
An Alternative View

> . . . panaceas tend to immobilize man at those moments
> when he ought to be exploring his alternatives creatively.
> *George Kelly, 1979, p. 64*

In the case studies in Chapter 4, we have shown how some
teachers and students use writing for learning. Some of the ways are
personal and have little to do with school or work. They make lists,
write notes to themselves and others, write letters, and keep journals.
This writing, by their own account, aids them in maintaining personal
relationships, in summarizing, remembering and communicating information or experiences, in exploring and mastering their feelings, in
applying their values, in furthering their understanding of the world,
and in taking action in the world.

Both teachers and students also use writing in school work.
The teacher's uses we might loosely call "instructional" and "professional." In their courses, they assign or require writing which is designed to help students focus on, clarify, think through, analyze
comment on, summarize, synthesize, infer from, generalize about,
and speculate about curriculum material. This writing is for instructional purposes and is, in a general way, intended to help students
find and solve problems in the discipline. The professional uses are
connected with committee work, student counseling, proposal writing, report writing, publishing, evaluating students and programs,
and the like.

The more universal student uses, which we call "curricular,"
include writing to outline, understand, reflect on, translate (from
subject language to everyday language, and vice versa), eliminate confusion, ask questions, organize material or thoughts, classify, differ-
entiate, document, interpret, self-test, expand upon, and remember.

172

To do this, students employ a variety of types of writing, from initial, sketchy notes, through rewrites of notes to informal drafts of
papers to formal, finished papers. This writing ranges from personal
to impersonal, from informal to formal, and from colloquial in style
to academic in style. *All* of this writing is important in two ways.
First, the teachers require (or encourage) this writing because they
see it as helpful for learning rather than for testing students' knowledge of nursing or psychology or entomology. Nor do the students
undertake the writing to display their knowledge for their teachers.
Both groups see the bulk of this writing as aiding learning. They
agree that successful learners develop the ability to see cause and
effect, find connections, discover implications, achieve shifts in
perception and take material learned in one area for use in another.
Second, the teachers and students value informal *and* formal writing,
as well as colloquial and academic style. They understand that the
learner's rephrasing of information into her own language reflects
that individual's reconstruction of knowledge. They are in the minority in this regard, as most teachers still discourage informal writing
in everyday language, approaching such language as if it evidenced
bad writing or bad students rather than learning in process.

While there are a few schools and colleges in every state in
which teachers and students are using writing in similar ɔntradi-
tional ways, mainstream writing practices, in other subjects as well
as in English, still present quite a different picture (Applebee, 1981;
Parker, 1985; Fillion, 1983). Teachers at all levels continue to use
writing to improve writing or to test knowledge. Moreover, rapid
increases in state-wide assessments of reading, math, and writing
competency are strengthening rather than weakening this tradition.
This testing lends impetus to the teaching of writing to improve
writing skill, not to the use of writing to improve learning about
self or world.

As for the pockets of alternative practice, if we take them to
reflect different theories-in-action, we can assume that alternative
views of learning and teaching lie beneath such practices. These alternative views of learning, whether explicitly or implicitly held,
accord quite closely with the views of language, thinking and learning which we discussed earlier in Chapters 1–3.

In the mainstream view of learning, learners are characterized
as receivers of knowledge, and essentially passive receivers at that.
Knowledge, already codified within disciplines, exists outside of
and apart from learners, mainly in teachers' minds and in textbooks.
The teachers' role is to transmit this knowledge directly to students
through talking and assigning reading, and the students' role is to
receive it. The research of Barnes and Shemilt (1975; see also Barnes,

1976) supports our claim. Most secondary teachers surveyed held
transmission views of language and knowledge, particularly those
teaching in the sciences and social sciences. They saw language as
simply transmitting preexisting, preformulated knowledge *from*
teachers *to* students. Students, they assume, learn passively by taking in such knowledge through listening and reading. Here is a com-
posite description of the "Transmission teacher":

> The Transmission teacher is primarily aware of writing as a
> means of measuring the pupil's performance against his own
> expectations and criteria. When he sets written work, his atten-
> tion is focused upon the kind of writing he wants, so that he is
> careful to ensure that his pupils understand what he wants of
> them. He assumes that it is his business to define the task for
> his pupils, and to provide them with information about their
> success in measuring up to his standards. He values writing as
> a record to which his pupils can later look back, but assumes
> they will address it to a general disembodied reader rather than
> to themselves or to him. He believes his main responsibility in
> receiving pupils' writing to be the awarding of a grade. Usually
> he continues with the lessons he has already planned, and does
> not refer back to pupils' previous work, which he regards as
> completed when he hands back his assessment to his pupils.
> On the occasions when he does mention pupils' work in class,
> he uses it either as a means of correcting errors in content or
> manner, or as an opportunity to emphasize to the class the
> need to preserve high standards of written work. On the whole
> he regards writing as a record for future reference rather than
> as a means of learning . . . (Barnes, 1976, p. 141)

Since the mid-1960s, many studies of classroom verbal interaction have been conducted. The findings about classroom talk,
from the elementary grades through college, support this description
of the "Transmission teacher" as reflecting the mainstream view of
the role of language in the teaching/learning process. Teachers initiate and control virtually all verbal interactions. They set topics and
structures of discussions, ask nearly all the questions, and provide
virtually all the evaluations of student responses. Two-thirds of the
time, on the average, someone is talking in most classrooms, and
two-thirds of that time the teacher is talking. By controlling the
topic, structure, and evaluation of all verbal interactions, teachers
control all the important meanings which are communicated and
used, and learning can be characterized as a process of students
moving into and taking on their teachers' meanings (Edwards and
Furlong, 1978).

Teachers not only ask most of the questions, they mostly ask factual questions in a search for correct answers. Often, teachers appear to be looking not just for correct answers, but for correct answers using a certain specific term (or terms). Even in humanities subjects, teachers seldom ask open-ended questions calling for such thinking operations as analyzing, synthesizing, hypothesizing, theorizing, or speculating. The actual questions teachers ask in discussions and in writing assignments consistently prohibit students from doing much higher order thinking of any sort. Obviously, teachers' theories-in-action suggest an underlying view of learning as a passive, receptive, fact-oriented process. Their classroom actions indicate little sense of the potential of either talking or writing as a means of thinking about or learning curriculum material. Language seems to exist only to transmit knowledge, not to construct or interpret it.

In an interim report on his research into the kinds of English teaching experienced by 11–12-year-old pupils in England, Peter Medway (1984) offers two relevant observations. Though his comments are about teaching English, the view of language and learning which they imply is, as we have been suggesting, widely shared among teachers of all subjects—as evidenced by the ways they structure, initiate, and respond to discussions, writing, and reading in their classrooms.

First,

> between writing which is about nonexistent realities, literature which is exclusively fiction and "language work" on bits of language which have been made up for the occasion and in which the appearance of empirical reference is illusory, it is possible for pupils to spend almost their whole time in English in some insubstantial limbo. The language may almost never engage with the facticity of an actual state of affairs. Indeed, the possibility of a language used heuristically as a means of interpreting and understanding, of making the world available to thought, does not seem to be allowed for in the prevailing implicit model of teaching. (p. 140)

The last part of his observation is crucial. Somehow, the real world is quite completely shut out of the classroom, and a substitute, fictionalized reality is created in its place. English work is about this substitute reality, guaranteeing that the pupils' activities will have no effects *in the world* — either of understanding or effecting it.

Rather, as his second observation suggests,

> pupils must be generating and receiving messages about which the important thing is not whether they tell you anything but

that they are the right sorts of messages, composed of prescribed categories of elements articulated to interact in preferred ways. Thus, for a teacher to direct the language outwards with the intention of penetrating the world is to . . . work against the grain. Attempts to make language the means to knowledge are difficult to sustain, so firmly is it built into the institution of English that language, not knowledge, is the end. (p. 140)

Here, Medway seems to capture the essential purpose of much written work in subjects other than English as well. In reporting on laboratory work in science classes, pupils are typically required to use a set format: slotting highly specified bits of information, using specific terminology, into rigidly specified categories (e.g., purpose, equipment, procedures, findings, conclusions). In social studies, certain kinds of essays and research papers are universally assigned. Here, too, the *purpose* of the writing seems to be mastery of these forms, including the accompanying research and bibliographic techniques. In neither subject is there much evidence that these written forms (or formats) are intended for pupils to use heuristically for penetrating the world. Language, not knowledge, is the end in these subjects as it is in English, and these uses of writing in science and social studies are unmarked cases also. How different this approach is from that taken by Professor Butchko in his entomology course.

And not only can language, used heuristically, provide the means of penetrating and understanding reality beyond the self, it can, as Ann E. Berthoff (1984) reminds us, become the means of examining those very understandings of the world which we have used language to construct in the first place. Language can, as she notes, become the means of interpreting our interpretations (from Kenneth Burke) and of "knowing our knowledge" (Coleridge). "Consciousness of consciousness is," in Berthoff's words, "entailed in our activity as language animals" (p. 747). "Yes," we would say in reply, "but not very often in schools. In fact, very, very seldom in schools." Mastery of forms, or language for the sake of language, derails language used to construct consciousness, let alone language used to construct consciousness of consciousness.

Our view of learners, language and learning contrasts sharply with this mainstream perspective. We see learners as active not passive, constructors of knowledge not receivers of knowledge. Through language (and other physical and symbolic means), they actively construct knowledge for themselves through their interactions with teachers, peers, textbooks, field experiences, and so forth. Unless students have a hand in *setting* topics for discussion or writing, unless they formulate open-ended questions which they are motivated to answer, unless they hypothesize, theorize, and speculate about curriculum material, they will not learn that material in any deep or permanent way. Learning requires active engagement in using language to inquire into and reflect upon the experience, information, or concepts presented in the curriculum and by the world.

Seen from this perspective, learners run thoughts through their minds, recycling them to embed the new information into existing knowledge — or "on the brain," as several of our informants said. Each recycling of material through the mind produces a further transformation of knowledge. These successive transformations are characterized by the use of seemingly contradictory processes, alone or in pairs. The first pair involves use of familiar, personal language together with the incorporation of more specialized subject-specific terms. These "languages" may be used concurrently or consecutively. The next pair includes the processes of expansion and contraction of material: contraction to its essence and expansion to include more detail. These processes can move toward analysis or toward synthesis and from superficial notation to reformulation in more formal terms as seen in the "writing to learn" strategies of the students in entomology, psychology, nursing, and mathematics.

We also see writing as a steppingstone to further thought and as an instrument for making connections with curriculum material and the world. Writing helps sharpen the learner's powers of observation, both as a cause and as a consequence. For some, writing serves as a valuable attention-getting or focusing device, enabling them "to key in [and] to listen" more intensely. For others, the value of writing lies in reading it over to discover intent and meaning.

Thus, learning always takes place through the person's internal reconstruction of interactional processes; it is not a commodity one person can get from another. What the person learns may be about the self or about the world. Regardless, learning occurs as people make connections, and it involves the intellectual operations of analysis and synthesis. Writing serves as a strategy for both.

This is truly an alternative theoretical perspective. It presents a view of how people learn and what role language plays in that process which conflicts with the current implicit paradigm. Because the perspectives are not compatible, teachers must choose one or the other. The old pseudo pragmatic adage, "I just take a little bit from this and a little bit from that — whatever works is all I care about," doesn't hold. We all must make a choice, especially as more politically conservative forces gain greater control of public school financing, curricula, and large-scale assessment procedures.

In actuality, most teachers have already made a choice. Most are already operating from one perspective or the other, and their choice of perspective was made long ago, while they were students. Whatever teacher preparation program they attended, they wanted methods of teaching to implement their a priori personal theories and a classroom in which to attempt the implementation.

None of this means that new or alternative theoretical perspectives on learning and teaching are irrelevant in teacher training. Quite the opposite. Because each teacher's theoretical perspective is crucial to the way she or he teaches, it is essential that the training process be designed to assist teachers in making explicit and taking responsibility for their implicit theories of teaching and learning. Once they have made their implicit theoretical perspectives explicit, and acknowledged them, these perspectives can be examined in the light of their historical and social roots (where these theories come from and whose interests they serve) *and* of alternative theories.

This process of examining personal, informal theories in the light of impersonal, formal theories has been described by Parker (1982b).

> Thus, learning involves a movement from experience to the personal viewpoints we construct, the result of which is personal "theory." Occasionally, we encounter THEORY, those more formal and abstract hypotheses about how large segments of the world work, or why they work as they do. We can make THEORY of this order a part of our world view only in relation to the personal theory we have constructed. So, from experience we construct a "theory," *in use*, and then move from its practical, ready-made hypotheses to the experts' hypotheses (THEORY) and back. (p. 414)

As with students, teachers (in training or in practice) are most fruitfully viewed as *constructors*, not *receivers*, of theories. Since they come to any training experience, whether pre- or in-service, with ready-to-hand theories, the training experience can be most fruitfully presented as one which will encourage them to become involved in *retheorizing* their teaching field. This retheorizing will arise from the transaction between their current personal perspectives and whatever new perspective is being offered in the training. If new methods are offered without theoretical rationale, they may or may not be tried out. If teachers try new methods out, and the methods are compatible with their existing perspective, they will probably be incorporated more or less permanently into those teachers' repertoires. If these methods are incompatible, they will be discarded — and no one, certainly not those teachers, will understand *why* either kind of action has been taken. "They work, that's all I know" is likely to be the explanation. That sort of explanation may be satisfactory for the current generation of anti-intellectual "bottom liners," but it is not satisfactory for a conscious, rational, intellectual profession like teaching.

In reviewing the language across the curriculum movement and commenting on its "potential for change," Nancy Martin observes that

> innovations in schools which are the result of a new theoretical position tend to be taken up as if they were just an alternative method, and the theoretical implications which could have more far-reaching results get lost. (1983, p. 104)

This, it seems to us, is what has happened to a great extent with WAC in the U.S. Though WAC *is* "the result of a new theoretical position," as we have attempted to show, it has been taken up across the country "as if [it] were just an alternative method." As a result, the implications, which are far-reaching have been lost by all but a few teachers (Barr, D'Arcy, Healy, 1982) and a few programs in high schools and colleges.

Training programs in WAC have not, generally, involved teachers in critical transactions between their a priori theories and the WAC theoretical perspectives. They have not made clear to teachers that retheorizing their teaching is more important, at the outset, than revamping their methods. They have not insisted that you don't have a WAC program when you haven't incorporated the theoretical ideas which underlie the movement. They have not suggested that methods *come from theory*, as logically derived implications, and that good theory provides a rich supply of good methods for implementation. There has been a failure in point of view and in nerve.

The original WAC proponents foresaw this kind of problem and resisted the efforts to "program" LAC and WAC. As James Britton argued eloquently, both theoretical ideas and research findings are "starting points" for teachers to use in working out their own applications and implementations. This book is presented in that light: as a series of starting points to use in working out your own most fruitful applications and implementations. Such development work is best done collaboratively, through ongoing discussions, classroom research, and curriculum experimentation with colleagues from various departments. From such involvement with WAC ideas about teaching and learning come new ways of teaching that genuinely harness the potential that writing holds for thinking and learning.

References

Adams, P. (Ed.). (1973). *Language in thinking.* Harmondsworth: Penguin.

Applebee, A. (1981). *Writing in the secondary school.* Urbana, IL: National Council of Teachers of English.

Armstrong, M. (1979). *Closely observed children.* London: Writers and Readers Collaborative.

Barnes, D. (1976). *From communication to curriculum.* Harmondsworth: Penguin.

Barnes, D., & Shemilt, D. (1975, June). Transmission vs. interpretation. *Educational Review.*

Barnes, D., & Todd, F. (1977). *Communication and learning in small groups.* London: Routledge & Kegan Paul.

Barnes, D., Britton, J., & Rosen, H. (1969). *Language, the learner and the school.* Harmondsworth: Penguin.

Barr, M., D'Arcy, P., & Healy, M. K. (1982). *What's going on?* Upper Montclair, NJ: Boynton/Cook.

Berthoff, A. E. (1984, December). Is teaching still possible? Writing, meaning and higher order reasoning. *College Composition and Communication 36*:8

Bissex, G. (1980). *GNYS AT WRK: A child learns to write and read.* Cambridge, MA: Harvard University Press.

Bolton, N. (1972). *The psychology of thinking.* London: Methuen.

Britton, J. (1970). *Language and learning.* Harmondsworth: Penguin.

Britton, J. (1971). What's the use? A schematic account of language functions. *Educational Review 23*:3

Britton, J. (1981). *Talking, writing, learning and teacher education.* St. Louis, MO: CEMREL, Inc.

Britton, J., Burgess, T., Martin, N., McLeod, A., & Rosen, H. (1975). *The development of writing abilities 11–18.* London: Macmillan.

Bruner, J. (1975). Language as an instrument of thought. In A. Davies (Ed.), *Problems in language and learning*. London: Heinemann.

Burgess, T. (1984). The question of English. In M. Meek & J. Miller (Eds.), *Changing English*. London: Ward Lock.

Calkins, L. (1983). *Lessons from a child*. Exeter, NH: Heinemann.

Davis, F., & Parker, R. (1978). *Teaching for literacy: Reflections on the Bullock report*. London: Ward Lock.

Dewey, J. (1971). *Experience and education*. New York: Collier Books.

Diamond, C. T. P. (1982, May). Teachers can change: A Kellyan interpretation. *Journal of Education for Teaching 8*:2.

Diamond, C. T. P. (1983). The use of fixed role therapy in teaching. *Psychology in the Schools 20*:1.

Edwards, A., & Furlong, V. (1978). *The language of teaching*. London: Heinemann.

Elbow, P. (1976). *Writing without teachers*. New York: Oxford University Press.

Fillion, B. (1983). Language across the curriculum. In *International encyclopedia of education: Research and studies*. Oxford: Pergamon Press.

Kelly, G. (1955). *The psychology of personal constructs: Volume 1*. New York: Norton.

Kelly, G. (1963). *A theory of personality*. New York: Norton.

Kelly, G. (1979). The autobiography of a theory. In B. Maher (Ed.), *Clinical psychology and personality*. Huntington, NY: Robert E. Krieger.

Knoblauch, C., & Brannon, L. (1983, September). Writing as learning through the curriculum. *College English 45*:5.

Langer, S. (1978). *Philosophy in a new key*. Cambridge, MA: Harvard University Press.

Lunzer, E., & Gardner, K. (Eds.). (1979). *The effective use of reading*. London: Heinemann.

Maimon, E., Belcher, G., Hearn, G., Nodine, B., & O'Connor, F. (1981). *Writing in the arts and sciences*. Boston: Winthrop.

Martin, N. (1980). *The Martin report*. Perth, Australia: Department of Education, Western Australia.

Martin, N. (1983). *Mostly about writing*. Upper Montclair, NJ: Boynton/Cook.

Martin, N., D'Arcy, P., Newton, B., & Parker, R. (1976). *Writing and learning across the curriculum 11-16*. London: Ward Lock.

Martin, N., D'Arcy, P., Newton, B., Smith, H., Medway, P., Goodson, I., Watts, S., & Shapland, J. (1983). *Writing across the curriculum pamphlets*. Upper Montclair, NJ: Boynton/Cook.

Mead, G. H. (1934). *Mind, self and society*. Chicago: University of Chicago Press.

Medway, P. (1980). *Finding a language: Autonomy and learning in school*. London: Writers and Readers Collaborative.

Medway, P. (1984). Doing teaching English. In M. Meek & J. Miller (Eds.), *Changing English*. London: Ward Lock.

Miller, J. (1982). The basics and the imagination. In G. Hillocks (Ed.), *The English curriculum under fire*. Urbana, IL: National Council of Teachers of English.

National Association for the Teaching of English. (1976) *Language across the curriculum: Guidelines for schools*. London: Ward Lock.

Newton, B. (1978). The learner's view of himself. In F. Davis & R. Parker (Eds.), *Teaching for literacy*. London: Ward Lock.

Odell, L. (1980, February). The process of writing and the process of learning. *College Composition and Communication 31*.

Parker, R. (1981). *Writing practices across the curriculum in one high school: A status survey*. Unpublished report, Rutgers University, New Brunswick, NJ.

Parker, R. (1982, January). Language, school and the growth of mind. *CEA Critic 44*:2.

Parker, R. (1982, December). Writing courses for teachers: From practice to theory. *College Composition and Communication 33*.

Parker, R. (1985, May). The language across the curriculum movement: A brief overview and bibliography. *College Composition and Communication 36*.

Piaget, J. (1975). *To understand is to invent*. New York: Viking Compass.

Piaget, J. & Inhelder, B. (1969). *The psychology of the child*. New York: Basic Books.

Polanyi, M. (1962). *Personal knowledge*. New York: Harper Torchbooks.

Polanyi, M. (1968). *The tacit dimension*. Garden City, NY: Anchor Books.

Rosen, C., & Rosen, H. (1973). *The language of primary school children*. Harmondsworth: Penguin.

Sapir, E. (1961). *Culture, language and personality*. Berkeley, CA: University of California Press.

Schneider, K. (1983, April 6). Writing and thinking. *Education Week*.

Smith, F. (1982). *Writing and the writer.* New York: Holt, Rinehart and Winston.

Sommers, N. (1982, May). Responding to student writing. *College Composition and Communication 33*:2.

Talk Workshop Group (Eds.). *Becoming our own experts.* London: Inner London Education Authority.

Tighe, M. A., & Koziol, S., Jr. (1982, Spring). Practices in the teaching of writing by teachers of English, social studies and science. *English Education 14*:2.

Torbe, M., & Medway, P. (1981). *The climate for learning.* London: Ward Lock.

Vygotsky, L. (1962). *Thought and language.* (G. Vakar, Trans.). Cambridge, MA: MIT Press.

Vygotsky, L. (1978). *Mind in society.* M. Cole, S. Scribner, V. J. Steiner, & E. Souberman (Eds.). Cambridge, MA: Harvard University Press.

Wells, G., Bridges, A., French, P., MacLure, M., Sinha, C., Walkerdine, V., & Wall, B. (1981). *Learning through interaction.* Cambridge, England: Cambridge University Press.